Long Live BACON!

Where The Hell Is My Bacon?

How an Innocent Pork Product
Conquered Employee Engagement
and Change Management at a
Large Midwestern Corporation

BETH ANNE CAMPBELL

WHERE THE HELL IS MY BACON?: HOW AN INNOCENT PORK PRODUCT CONQUERED EMPLOYEE ENGAGEMENT AND CHANGE MANAGEMENT AT A LARGE MIDWESTERN CORPORATION

1405 SW 6th Avenue • Ocala, Florida 34471 • Phone 352-622-1825 • Fax 352-622-1875
Website: www.atlantic-pub.com • Email: sales@atlantic-pub.com
SAN Number: 268-1250

Library of Congress Cataloging-in-Publication Data

Names: Campbell, Beth Anne, author.
Title: Where the hell is my bacon? : how an innocent pork product conquered employee engagement and change management at a large midwestern corporation / by Beth Anne Campbell.
Description: Ocala, Florida : Atlantic Publishing Group, Inc., [2019] | Includes bibliographical references. | Summary: "Where The Hell Is My Bacon? is a polygamous marriage between business, fried pork, and humor. It is the story of a stressed out, disenfranchised technology department going through some very difficult changes at work that found their voice through bacon. *WTHIMBacon* is based on the true story of a protest that arose when a corporate health directive was issued at a large corporation, resulting in bacon bits being removed from the cafeteria salad bar. Although the book contains a lot of humor, it also brings important messages about leadership, employee engagement, communication, and trust"—Provided by publisher.
Identifiers: LCCN 2019051136 | ISBN 9781620237021 (paperback) | ISBN 9781620237038 (ebook)
Subjects: LCSH: Employee morale. | Personnel management. | Organizational change. | Bacon—Humor.
Classification: LCC HF5549.5.M6 C36 2019 | DDC 658.3/14—dc23
LC record available at https://lccn.loc.gov/2019051136

Printed in the United States

PROJECT MANAGER: Meaghan Summers
INTERIOR LAYOUT AND JACKET DESIGN: Nicole Sturk

Over the years, we have adopted a number of dogs from rescues and shelters. First there was Bear and after he passed, Ginger and Scout. Now, we have Kira, another rescue. They have brought immense joy and love not just into our lives, but into the lives of all who met them.

We want you to know a portion of the profits of this book will be donated in Bear, Ginger and Scout's memory to local animal shelters, parks, conservation organizations, and other individuals and nonprofit organizations in need of assistance.

– Douglas & Sherri Brown,
President & Vice-President of Atlantic Publishing

Table of Contents

Preface

A dark shadow had fallen over the technology department of a large Midwestern utility company. Five hundred geeks and nerds were drowning in a perfect storm of poorly managed corporate changes, paralyzing uncertainty, plummeting morale, and record-high job dissatisfaction. In the past year, they had weathered a brand new executive team that didn't understand them, a major reorganization that confounded them, and a massive outsourcing effort that had most of the department terrified of losing their jobs and sanity. While the new and ever-revolving management team attempted to appease the unrest with token "Team Building" gestures, the team sank further into hopelessness. They were defeated. The once-strong work family had been thrown into a black hole of change that sucked the life out of most of the department.

Then, one chilly November afternoon, an unexpected sun shone upon the techies as they slouched behind their cubicle walls. Their cold, despondent eyes slowly turned upward, and the glimmer of a once-forgotten dream reflected like dual 23-inch monitors onto their dejected faces. In an instant, there was hope. The IT department had found salvation, and its name was Bacon.

Disclaimer

The names in this tale have been changed to protect the innocent, which would mainly be me. I have made every attempt to not give people fake names that are lame or unpronounceable, or not in a million years what they might have been called if they had had different parents. The excerpts from our social media site are as close to the original comments as I can remember based on my journaling at the time and a little foresight that this unique time might someday still be important. I did correct a few grammar and spelling errors so people who recognize themselves won't be embarrassed and so you, the reader, won't think Information Technology people are way overpaid given their occasional lack of skills in written English.

Introduction

I am not a CIO, CEO, CFO, director, executive, or even upper or middle manager. I don't sit on the Board of Directors. I don't have a PhD or even an MBA. I have never won the Pulitzer Prize. In fact, other than a personal blog and some really amazing LinkedIn articles, I am barely a writer in the professional sense of the word. I have a modest house and drive a modest car, and my floors are badly in need of a cleaning. I failed out of a major university the first time I tried it and didn't get my bachelor's degree in business until I was 33 years old. I am definitely no Sheryl Sandberg or Bill Gates.

But I do know my bacon. And I know my people.

For nearly a decade, I was a first-level supervisor for a small group of analysts at a large Midwestern utility company. I started with the company as a programmer/developer writing code in the middle of the tech explosion in the early 2000s. I am not sure if I complained too much about coding or whether my astute boss saw something in me ready to blossom (or explode), but, after a couple of years in the programmer chair, he gave me my first technical lead assignment. Projects got bigger and bigger, and my assignments came with increasing responsibility until, one day, I found myself in a new role as a slightly—mostly—reluctant team manager.

This story of an unexpected bacon revolution does not come from someone high on the business food chain who is an undisputed master of change. This is a story from normal people, the ones in the depths of the corporate ocean—the bottom feeders, the doers of the planet, the ones who keep the world churning. These people told the powers that be what was wrong and demanded they make things better. They revolted against the constant silos of change happening around them, changes they did not understand, did not ask for, and in many cases had good reason to think were not the right thing to do. They spoke in a way they knew well: through humor and through food. If nothing else, this is a stark but very simple lesson to those high up on the management food chain: If you want to know what is wrong with your company, just ask. If you want to know how to fix your company, just ask. The people … they will tell you.

Chapter One

A Sad Day For Bacon

Bacon, how do I love thee? Let me count the ways:
I love thee in BLTs on warm summer days.

Darrin Potter: I was just told that bacon bits were removed from the salad bar in the cafeteria due to their low nutritional value. It's a sad day for bacon.

NOVEMBER 8 AT 12:36 P.M.

I rarely had an actual lunch break that November. In fact, it was still officially summer the last time I had been able to relax at my desk for half an hour over an egg salad sandwich or pretzel with mustard. As a self-proclaimed food-aholic, skipping a meal altogether was out of the question. But there was an undeniable need to use my lunch "hour" to catch up on unread emails or overdue tasks while I frantically chewed mediocre cafeteria food (or worse, the "Rack o' Death" vending machine alternative). Leaving the building was not an option, because the next corporate fire drill was just around the corner. A few months ago, a noontime de-stressor at the local Wendy's or Locos Rancheros across the street was a luxury my coworkers and I enjoyed on a regular basis. That was before I had been assigned as a lead in The Outsourcing Project From Hell. Sadly, I would not see my beloved redheaded, pig-tailed girl or a giant beef burrito again for many moons. But, after the chaos and turmoil of the past 60 days, even a mere 20 minutes to myself at my desk—without meetings, without inter-ruption—was like winning the lottery.

For over a decade, I worked in the Information Technology department of a large Midwestern utility company. A few years earlier, I transferred into the position commonly known as *The Team Lead*, a.k.a. "first-level super-visor." Or, as it became known to me, "the worst job in the world." OK, maybe not the worst, but, seriously, if anyone ever approaches you and asks if you want to be a manager … flee. Channel your inner cheetah and sprint your ass out of that conversation before another word is spoken. I would be lying if I said I embraced the role—far from it. Prior to management, I had been a successful "doer" focused on a finite number of roles for a manageable quantity of high-profile projects and seeing them through to great success. I went from a coder to a technical lead on small assignments, to a technical lead on large efforts, playing just about every project role out there. And I found great satisfaction as my career progressed.

As it sometimes happens, the people who work their way to success often get promoted to managerial positions. For many of them, this is a great fit. They easily fall into a role where they can find achievement and self-fulfill-ment through the accomplishments of other people. They learn to delegate the tasks they once excelled at to their team members and smoothly move onto a higher level of responsibility. I envy those people, but I am not one of them. I took on the responsibility of manager with full respect, don't get me wrong. But I am an inherently selfish person and was unwilling to give up performing those self-satisfying assignments myself. Delegation was something I had to work on for a long time, because I was accustomed to—and very much liked—being a doer versus a manager. I didn't know how to find success through others. And, if I am being honest, I liked the recognition. But I eventually learned to (sort of) embrace the manage-rial career path looming in front of me. I soon settled down into what I thought would be a steady, comfortable lane.

Three years into my management journey, everything changed.

Just about a year BB (Before Bacon), our department got a new chief infor-mation officer named Maya Chad. Maya was quite different from the last CIO. Actually, I can't even say for certain that we *had* a CIO before Maya came on board. If we did, he was a ninja CIO, because I don't even know if he was really a "he" or what he/she/they looked like, and I certainly never spoke to her—or them.

One of the first things Maya did was put the department through a major reorganization within a few months of her arrival. Goliath-like would be a good way to describe it. My opinion—and I believe one of many experts, none of whom I will use as a primary source, other than to say I did read this in a Gartner article once—is that reorgs should be done *only when absolutely necessary.* They should not be one of the first things a manager or director or vice president or CIO does after they are hired unless the situation is dire. There is a period of time during which you have to earn your employees' trust. People have a difficult time with change, especially significant change. When you put them through a difficult time without understanding them and without working your way gently into their trust zone, it appears as if you don't value them. When they don't feel valued, they become unhappy. Unhappiness is like a disease that spreads through-out the company, and the symptoms are lower productivity, lack of moti-vation, plummeting morale, and a kind of chaotic soup that pervades the workplace. Reorganization is a major change. Do the math.

The second thing Maya did, less than a year after her arrival, was announce that the IT department would be outsourced to an offshore team in India. Well, I'm sure you can imagine how well *that* went over.

In between these two major spirit-crushing events, there were small sparks of goodness, such as when Maya opened employee access to several social media sites that had previously been blocked on our corporate network: Yammer, Facebook, and Twitter.

Yammer is an application very similar to Facebook, but for businesses. You can post statuses, comment, "like," and create groups just like you can on the more well-known social site (to which I happen to be highly addicted … "like" if you are, too). It was one way to drag our draconian policies out of the Middle Ages, and, like many of my coworkers, I was drawn to the social site like I'm drawn to Reese's Peanut Butter cups. And, if you could see my ass, you'd know what I was talking about.

Most of the chatter on Yammer was very businesslike. Maya herself posted regularly, and even some of our other old-school executives had taken up using this social marvel. Of course, whenever the vice presidents, directors, and upper managers start posting, the ass-kissers are never far behind. I can't knock Yammer, because it was a venue for communication we had not experienced before. But most of the content was "rah-rah, look how great of a company we are, life is great!" Technology! Entertainment! Design! Oh wait, that's TED. Technology! Innovation! Business! *Look at me, I just posted another LinkedIn article called "The Seven Things Good Managers Do To Keep Their Minions Under Control!" Hey, check out this new tablet review from mashable.com! I agree with you 100 percent, Mr. Vice-President, now please bend over and drop your executive drawers while I virtually pucker up!*

The onslaught of posts on how great we were for entering the 21st century—long after it had started—just made some of us roll our eyes as we saw our department crumbling around us. Yammer and the other social media outlets were a distraction. They were positive on the surface, but, in retrospect, seemed like ploys to get people's minds off the outsourcing and discord, blinding us to what was really going on with our jobs. I'm sure the company was following some formula a brilliant research psychoanalyst business expert came up with to handle major, unwanted change at a large corporation.

"First … " they would say—I imagine in a European accent, maybe German or the Queen's English—"distract the employees with 'gifts' that appear to be rewards for their good behavior. Allow them access to some things they didn't have before (harmless things, of course, no sense in going overboard with the trust and responsibility. After all, they are mere worker bees). Social media, for example. They'll think you are a god.

"Then start inviting some low-level employees—team leads, first-level supervisors, maybe even a promising worker bee him- or herself—to consult with you … *as if* you really care what they think. Pretend to listen and agree with their 'great' ideas, which you can promptly ignore. Allow them to pursue innovative ideas (à la 3M) as long as they do it on their own time, because the regular work won't stop. (It's actually going to get much worse, but don't tell them that!) Pretend to empathize with the huge workload they are all carrying so they come to believe it's something they cannot handle. All the while, carefully and gradually start talking about outsourcing. But for goodness' sake, don't call it 'outsourcing!' We don't want it to sound as bad as it really is. Let's call it 'managed sourcing' and then find a way to make it seem as if 'managed sourcing' is really the savior to rescue all of the employees from the ugly workload that they can't possibly keep up with. Yes, we know they have done this so far, but we want them to believe they are overworked and that bringing in an outsourcing … er, rather, a 'managed sourcing' team … will relieve them of this burden. All clear? Excellent, now GO!"

All that being said, we sure did like our Yammer. Along with the ass-kissing, boring business posts and numerous uses of Yammer as a pseudo-help desk, there were occasional bright spots. A few of us rebellious types always took advantage of any opportunity to add some levity. Mingled in with the corporate mush were pockets of brilliance, like dog stories and lots of sarcastic humor. But, for the most part, it was simply another mechanism to talk about boring work stuff.

Oddly enough, it was on Yammer where we found bacon and our salvation.

In that now-renowned November, sitting at my desk for an unprecedented power lunch, I wasn't even thinking about bacon. I mean, of course I was thinking about bacon. What self-respecting non-vegetarian doesn't think about pork products at least 187 times per day? What I meant was I wasn't thinking about bacon as a beacon of change. At that point, bacon was just a fleeting thought in my nebulous brain, like "I need to go to the bathroom" or "It feels good to stretch." Sometimes I would get up to go to the bathroom and a slab of thick-cut, apple-smoked bacon would flash into my mind like an awesome, instantaneous daydream. When I stood up from my desk to stretch—as one should do at least every hour or so—I might hear sizzling in the back of my brain. But I didn't really think about bacon consciously, as one might think about making a doctor's appointment or finishing an internet quiz (in case you were wondering, the *Lord of the Rings* character I am most like is Aragorn).

As I popped open a bag of Cheetos (lunch of champions), I decided to check my Yammer feed. I wasn't expecting much, but, as a one-time power-user of this social mecca, I missed it desperately. A few months earlier, I had been on several leader boards for Most Likes and Most Comments (*thank yuh ... thank yuh very much*), but, after my long absence, I thought I might have been forgotten.

And then, there it was, right at the top of my news feed, posted just seconds before my login. Bacon. Oh, you scamp, you. Where have you been all this time?

> **Darrin Potter:** I was just told that bacon bits were removed from the salad bar in the cafeteria due to their low nutritional value. It's a sad day for bacon. ☹
>
> NOVEMBER 8 AT 12:36 P.M.

WHAT? Was this a post that did not involve congratulating a vice president on an important executive decision? A post not asking a help desk question, or giving kudos to an intern for pulling an all-nighter to get through a project? A post about nothing businesslike at all, revolving around my favorite pork product EVER? I don't believe in fate, but this was most definitely fate. On any other day, I would have missed this gem. It would have been buried under mountains of the business mundane, and we would have never crossed paths. But there it was, in black and white, staring me in the face on the first day I had logged into Yammer in months. And I was on it like honey on a hot biscuit.

I knew the pain from whence Darrin spoke. A couple of weeks earlier, a corporate edict had been handed down to the cafeteria, designed to make it more difficult—or impossible—to buy unhealthy food. I have no doubt this mandate came partly from concerns about growing healthcare costs, and partly from someone's genuine commitment to improving the health of us physically substantial types who consider a Snickers bar a well-rounded meal (it has nuts, and nuts have *fiber*). As a logical, reasonable person with a higher-than-average IQ (so I tell myself), I could actually comprehend the motive behind this move. However, as a resident truffle-shuffler with a high-er-than-average appetite, I was, like, "ARE YOU FOR REAL, BITCH??? A DOLLAR EXTRA FOR REAL FREAKING CHEESE?!"

Let me digress here for a moment. Someone please define for me what "healthy" is by cafeteria standards (or any standards, for that matter). They removed bacon from the salad bar, yet all the non-organic, pesticide-laden vegetables remained. They charged extra for regular soda pop versus diet, because sugar is apparently *so* much worse for you than artificial sweeteners that ravage your endocrine system. They made us pay more for real cheddar made from actual milk and less for fake cheddar made from hydrogenated oil. Antibiotic-laden chicken burgers were served on top of gut-inflaming, refined white flour buns. The concept of "healthy" is quite subjective, my friends. Just check the news. For the life of me I can't recall if coffee is good for me or bad for me this week. Or eggs. The crowning moment was when they started charging extra if we wanted cheese … on a quesadilla. A que-sadilla, in case you didn't know, is a CHEESE DILLA! Queso = cheese! By definition, it contains cheese! That's like charging extra if you want bacon on your BLT! It's not a BLT if you don't get the *B*! Critical thinking skills are so important.

Now, back to our tale, still in progress. Bacon post. Yammer. Angels singing.

But wait! What just happened? The bacon post was gone! Oh Darrin, Dar-rin, no … what the hell? This cannot be happening. I cannot be denied my one chance in a million to talk about crackling, fatty-lard pig! Oh, no you didn't!

I popped out of my chair, almost slamming into my cubicle wall (OK, "wall" is probably stretching it) and ran over to the next aisle where Darrin sat. Despite the fact that I would be losing precious minutes of a lunch break I barely had anyway, this was a mission. Darrin sat at his desk with his hand on the mouse, the blood from his deleted pork post still warm.

"Dude!" I cried, because that's how professional managers talk. "Dude, what happened to the bacon post? I was just about to comment!"

I'm sure Darrin could see the desperate, crazed look in my eyes. Fortunately, Darrin is very smart, so he did not call company security. He shrugged his shoulders sheepishly and muttered some lame excuse about second thoughts and not wanting to offend people in the cafeteria. Blah blah blah. I was not having it. There is no excuse for denying bacon.

"Seriously, you will not offend anyone," I reassured him. I like to think I have a strong emotional intelligence. I knew bacon was just what we needed right then, because I knew people like their bacon and they like their choices. "I promise you, if you post it again I will 'like' and comment right away in full support."

I made some attempt at a pseudo-Scout's Honor motion with my fingers on my forehead even though I wasn't really a scout, and it probably looked more like I was brushing away a fly than giving a solid oath. But it worked, because Darrin agreed to re-post his bacon complaint.

Victory. Is. Mine.

I hustled back to my seat and started typing.

> **Beth Anne Campbell in reply to Darrin Potter:** I'm glad I'm not the only one. By the way, stress is one of the top unhealthy things in the universe, and I'm pretty sure the AMA approved both bacon and chocolate as recommended supplements for their calming effects. Everything in moderation. Bring back the pig.
>
> NOVEMBER 8 AT 12:38 P.M.

Sarcasm. It's just one of the services I offer.

I must pause here for a moment because some of you may be going through your own company-mandated health kick. Let me reassure you, *this too shall pass*. I have lived through four or five of these in my two decades in the corporate world, and every time it is the same: they remove some of the "unhealthy" foods altogether and charge more for anything left that Corporate deems questionable. Sales, of course, will plummet. Then, inevitably they restore said "unhealthy" foods and have happy employees once again. This will happen in your organization, so just deal with it by heading to the local Mexican restaurant for lunch where you can ride it out with extra sour cream and medium salsa (which contains, as it were, many healthy vegetables).

> **Beth Anne Campbell in reply to Darrin Potter:** Also, is the recent healthy overhaul the reason why the coffee counter has not had those DELECTABLE cookies this week? This may cause a riot. If I can't have the occasional giant white chocolate macadamia soft, home-baked, scrumptious cookie, I might just have to start OCC (Occupy Corporate Cafe).
>
> NOVEMBER 8 AT 12:50 P.M.
>
> LIKED BY CASSIE TAMARACK, JEN PARKER, AND CAROL BURNS

This all took place around the time Occupy Wall Street was peaking. And this is in no way intended to seriously compare the missing white chocolate macadamia giant soft home-baked scrumptious cookies with the real Occupy movement. As AMAZING as those cookies were, and as distressing as it was when they disappeared, they did not compare to the real struggles of real people facing real corporate greed. Apples and oranges, people.

I found out later that the cookies had NOT, in fact, been removed as part of the health mandate. The kitchen cooks were simply running behind. Which, I think, underscores my earlier point. Remove bacon but leave the diabetes disks? Sugar causes far more damage to our bodies than bacon ever will, even in its fattiest, most nitrate-saturated form. As astounding as bacon is, I don't walk past the meat section at the grocery store thinking that I absolutely must have a package of Oscar Mayer hickory-smoked bacon RIGHT NOW in the same way I do a Twix or Kit Kat bar in the checkout aisle. Sugar is a different beast altogether, and, although I don't want to give the vice president who dealt out this health directive any ideas, removing desserts would have been a more logical alternative.

It didn't take long for others in the department to recognize what an atrocity it was to ban an innocent pork product from the salad bar.

> **Bart Swartout in reply to Darrin Potter:** This is all a bit too authoritarian for me. I am all for having healthy choice options, but removing arguably "bad" choices altogether seems a little radical. I mean, who really wants to eat salad unless it's flavored up with bacon and a healthy portion of grated cheddar? No one is the answer. I get this makes it "less healthy," but it allows me to tolerate the kale, bean sprouts, and mushrooms. Without those little bits of paradise we call bacon, I will just head over to Wendy's and get myself a Baconator. Which kind of defeats the purpose of removing bacon bits in the first place.
>
> NOVEMBER 8 AT 1:04 P.M. FROM IPAD
> LIKED BY BETH ANNE CAMPBELL, TAMARA BRYAN, RODNEY CARTER, AND
> FOUR OTHERS

Bart's participation in this chain of comments is critical, because he was higher up than me on the managerial food chain. OK, nearly any manager was above me on the corporate hierarchy, but even one level higher gives much more credibility to our lost bacon laments. Plus, Bart was the golden boy of the IT department—really smart, quick, and with an eye for innovation. When he left to go work for another utility company in Texas two years AB (After Bacon) and just after our CIO Maya left the company, it is rumored one of our vice presidents gave Bart not only his personal cell phone number but also his wife's personal cell phone number. Allegedly, he told Bart to get a couple years' experience, and he'd bring him back to fill the vacated CIO seat. That didn't end up happening, but Bart was so well

known and respected in the IT department, some of us believed it could
be true.

And so, within 30 minutes of Darrin's original post, his worries about bacon shredding the morale of the cafeteria staff were proven unfounded. In
two days, it would become the all-time most commented on post in our
company's Yammer history. And, within a week, it would spawn a protest
that painted a clearer portrait of the gaps in the department's change management and employee engagement efforts than the powers that be ever
could … or did.

Chapter Two

Job Whack-a-Mole

I love thee in omelets and eggs scrambled hot;
I love thee in chili I cook in a pot.

A few months earlier, bacon was the furthest thing from my thoughts.

OK, that's a lie. Bacon is always on the periphery, but my life was so disorganized and chaotic that the electrical connections in my brain were sputtering like bad spark plugs. I was incapable of coming to the normal, logical conclusion that any situation could be helped by frying some fatty pork. There were so many things happening at work that most of us could hardly think straight. Our new CIO was bringing in a refreshing outlook on technology, driving us towards innovation and opening our work lives to social media … while, at the same time, scaring the shit out of us with the nonsensical reorganization and the outsourcing initiative. Sorry, forgive me—*managed sourcing* initiative. It was difficult to accept this direction was the right way to go when actions seemed to conflict with words, and our concerns remained ignored. Additionally, projects were piling up, and that meant work was piling up. All of this, coupled with a major reorg, uncertainty, and the executive management team's inability to connect to their people, made for some very, very tough times.

It is important to understand the mindset during this time. We hadn't even started prepping for the managed sourcing effort in earnest yet, and people were already confused about their roles. No one understood what they were going to be doing. And roles were in constant flux. I personally went through four job changes in less than a month over the summer, and, although I may have been somewhat of an extreme example, my situation was by no means rare. But, in the interest of discovering why and how an innocent utility supervisor became the company Queen of Bacon and why the masses were so easily roused, my job merry-go-round is as good an example as any.

Assignment 1: Team Lead for the Work and Asset Administration (WAA) Team

Before all the outsourcing and reorg madness began, I was leading my team of sunshine and rainbows. None of the other roles really mattered at this point. I had been with this team for almost three years, and we were close, like cousins who lived next door to each other. Even before we became a cohesive team during a previous reorg, most of us had been working together on projects for years. So, making it official on paper was a fluid transition. It was with Team WAA that I learned to not hate being a manager. We had come to a comfortable place as a well-oiled machine in our duties taking care of one of our largest and most critical systems in the company.

Assignment 2: Team Lead for the Geospatial Information Systems (GIS) Team

The Job Change Whack-a-Mole game started not long before the managed sourcing initiative was scheduled to kick off and just a few months *BB*. My boss Dan pulled me into one of many impromptu meetings we had to talk about our department organization. We had far, far too many organization discussions. It was clearly a problem. Dan wanted to discuss the org structure for his handful of teams. The new boxes in his presentation were all too familiar, blurring in my brain with the other, similar boxes I had reviewed four or five times in the past couple of years. However, in this version there was one striking difference: I was no longer listed as Team Lead for WAA. What? Separated from my minions? We were like a little semi-dysfunctional family! Instead, he had placed me as head of another, sister team: *Geospatial Information Systems, or GIS*.

The GIS Team managed a number of critical, high-profile applications using geographical (or location-based) data, along with their technical framework. I knew the people on the GIS team well and had worked with a few of them on projects over the years. But unlike WAA, I had very little experience with most of the software they supported. Furthermore, the team itself had been somewhat unstable, having gone through a couple of temporary supervisors in the past few years. They had also seen an exodus of a few key team members to other departments and were strapped for resources—too much work, too little availability. This did not bode well for me, going from an established, comfortable team to one perceived as a little unsteady, challenged, and needing some work. I asked Dan if I was being punished. He thought I was joking and claimed he wanted someone strong in the role to help bring some structure to the team. They had been through a lot, were overworked, and he thought I could help.

This is how managers trick their employees into not fleeing from challenges like my dog flees from bath time. They flatter them. *Oh! I get it! You picked me because I'm AWESOME!* In truth, usually they just can't find anyone who wants the job. But to his credit, it worked. I drank the Kool-Aid. I liked the guys on the team, and I *did* want to help.

Because of my new GIS team lead role, I was scheduled for a business trip to California with a few of my new techno-geek team members. Bonus! The purpose of the trip was to work on some innovation ideas with one of our software venders (because that's what we were supposed to be doing under the new CIO leadership of Maya Chad, even though no one had time to innovate). I won't even pretend I had a clue of what the goal of this trip was ... not an inkling. But it was a paid trip to California and a break from the fire and brimstone of supervisor-ship, so I welcomed the opportunity and packed my bags.

Assignment 3: Project Manager for Carl's Happy Project

Two weeks before I left for the west coast, Dan called me into his office. Again.

"So, I've been thinking about this org chart," he began, pulling another printout from a neat pile on his desk. "I think I'm going to have Carl lead the Project From Hell for our department."

He didn't really call it Project From Hell. Its official name was EGCI, which stood for Employee Growth & Contracting Initiative, a.k.a., "*managed sourcing,*" a.k.a. the dreaded outsourcing project. The goal of this effort was to pass on our vast and deep knowledge of the systems we had basically helped build from the ground up onto a team of inexpensive offshore contractors who had a turnover percentage close to my actual age. We were supposed to hand over our systems to them for operational support and maintenance so we could "*have more time for important projects.*" Hindsight is 20/20. I can tell you for certain this absolutely did not happen for a lot of the department. At the time, though, we just didn't know. We wanted to believe, but it was difficult not to have nightmares about the possibility of a strange team coming in and taking over our responsibilities while we, despite promises to the contrary, were weeded out. We were lost. This was Maya's baby. Unfortunately, this baby was stinky, messy, it cried a lot, and none of the siblings really wanted it. Kind of like my youngest brother. BOOM! Just kidding, Chris.

I stared at my boss, silent and unblinking, across his desk of neatly placed office supplies. Dan's mid-level manager office had four actual walls and a door and was the exact opposite of my team lead cubicle, which had two half-walls and often smelled of day-old curdling hot cocoa. The hot cocoa was from my coffee. The magic of caffeine is obliterated by the grotesque, battery-acid taste of coffee, and there is no better way to mask it than with milk chocolate sweetness. Don't judge. Dan stacked papers neatly on his desk and had pictures of his smart, beautiful daughters on a shelf. I stacked coffee stains and soda pop cans and had sticky note reminders like "Don't be a bitch today … unless you have to" and "Bitter is not attractive."

"Um, OK, sure, that's fine, I guess," I responded somewhat hesitantly, not sure what Carl's new assignment had to do with me. Well, it wasn't fine for Carl, poor guy. Carl Knight is an awesome employee: bright guy, nice, hard worker. He deserved better. Sometimes, when we were in meetings together, I'd mutter a borderline inappropriate comment like "that's what she said" and look over to see Carl silently laughing when no one else got it. He's the kind of guy I would not have wished this EGCI thing on in a million years. I knew he would be great at it; it was just a shitty gig. Plus, he already had a big project he was leading.

"I think Carl would be perfect," I said. "But then who would be leading his other project?"

(Let's call his other project *Carl's Happy Project*.)

Dan replied, "Well, I was thinking you."

Wait, what? Dan, I just got a new supervisor job. I have a new team to whip into shape. Now you want me to take on *Carl's Happy Project*? Where's the hidden camera? Am I being PUNKED?

"We can have Carl transition his knowledge to you before you leave, and then you take over when you get back from the California trip."

I paused to reflect, which is to say dig my way out of the cesspool of confusion. "Uh, OK. I mean, I can do that, but I can't lead a massive project and a brand new team at the same time."

"No, I agree," said Dan. "Richard can stay on as the GIS Team Lead for a while longer until Carl's project is implemented."

Richard Chambers is a super-smart GIS solution architect who took over as manager for the GIS team temporarily after the previous reorg about a year earlier (I told you reorgs were a problem). Richard is a brilliant techie, and not a bad leader, but he did not want the role. He took it as a short-term solution, but it was clear it wasn't what he wanted to do in the long run. And, frankly speaking, his talent was wasted in a managerial position. I silently apologized to Richard, knowing he would not embrace this extension. He was probably already planning a celebration for his last day as a manager, and now I was going to be raining on his parade. Total monsoon.

"So, wait … what about California?" I asked.

If my role upon return was not leading the GIS Team, then it didn't make a whole lot of sense to take this trip. The trip was specifically for GIS stuff. It also didn't make much sense to pull Carl off a project he had been on for over six months, have him spend a lot of time transitioning everything to me, and then put both of us in unfamiliar territory whilst leaving at least one team of analysts with a temporary supervisor. But, as it turned out, since I would eventually be leading the GIS Team at some point down the road—and, more importantly, since the plane ticket was non-refundable—I was still going to California on the company dime. Who was I to argue? I mean, they don't have mosquitos in California. Not really.

So, are we keeping up? At this point, I am now officially on my third role in as many weeks, as project manager for *Carl's Happy Project*. Carl is now the lead for our area on the outsourcing Project From Hell. And Richard stays on in a managerial role for the GIS Team.

A couple of days before I left for the west coast, I begged Dan to reconsider. Doing the whirlwind knowledge transfer of *Carl's Happy Project* from Carl to me wasn't working out as planned. Six months of full-time progress doesn't just get from one brain to the other by osmosis (take note, outsourcing leadership). Plus, I still had to manage my current team (WAA) until this mess was final, which was more than a full-time job in itself. Carl was ramping up to start the EGCI/Project From Hell effort in a couple of weeks, and, with me being gone for a week on my business-paid vacation, I knew something would suffer. Fortunately, Dan is a wise man, and he agreed. So, he cancelled his edict for Job Switch #3. I was no longer Project Manager for *Carl's Happy Project*. I was now back to Role #2: Fearless Leader for the GIS Team.

So, at the end of this round of "Wheel of Positions" I was back on the "Managing a New Team" wagon. Although I knew it would be a challenge, I actually felt good about it. Certainly, making the California trip seemed more justified now, and I was back in my semi-comfort zone of being a reluctant first-level supervisor. Plus, Richard would be so happy. You're welcome.

Assignment 4: Hell Freezes Over

I was three days into my excursion in the humidity-free glory of the Golden State when I got a call from Dan during one of our GIS innovation brainstorming sessions. I had a feeling this would not be good as soon as I saw his name pop up on my work cellphone. Dan was a great boss, and he didn't call me unless he had to. I prayed it wasn't a crisis to pull me away from this energized, motivated group of sassy young-ish nerds whose mojo was highly contagious. But my prayers were not answered (again), and this is why I don't go to church.

Dan's message was not good. It was another assignment change, and this time he told me he wanted me—not Carl—to lead the dreaded outsourcing project for our area.

NO! NO, GOD, NO, NO, NO!!!

The Project From Hell fell into my lap, and I swear there were burn marks on my pants.

I was sitting across the table from the California company's account manager, Rick Higgins, and I think it was clear from my expression that the news from the other end of the phone was not pleasant. I was floored. I had gone through four job changes in as many weeks—five if you count the cancelled one—and could barely keep it together at the table. The stress of the constant change was bad enough, but now it was like I was being punished. I felt like a straight-A valedictorian getting sent to a rough juvenile home.

Rick was watching me cautiously. Rick has a high degree of emotional intelligence, and he can read people well. What he was reading on my face that day was something between *I'm gonna lose my shit on someone today* and *someone just took away my bacon.*

"Well," I managed to choke out after I hung up my phone. "Apparently I am not going to be managing the GIS Team when I get back. I am going to be leading the Project From Hell for our portfolio."

Rick nodded silently, in full understanding and heartfelt sympathy. He was a great account representative and very much a part of our family even though we had different employers. He totally got it. He had seen similar outsourcing efforts happening at many of the companies he worked with. He understood my pain. Because, who would really WANT to lead this effort?

Hi, how ya doin'? Yeah, so, I don't really understand this program, not entirely sure what it means for my job, don't really believe the executives who say "no one will be fired," kinda feeling super-unengaged as it is, believe work life is a circus on steroids, but, hey … I would LOVE to help out. Sign me up to lead the knowledge transition of our support areas—software solutions and technologies we helped build from the ground up in which we take absolute pride and ownership as if they were our CHILDREN—and fork it over in a matter of months to a bunch of strangers who live and work across the planet. OOH, OOH, MISTUH KOTTAH! CALL ON ME! I can't think of anything more fulfilling. Can you feel my employee engagement skyrocketing as you read this?

That was sarcasm, in case you aren't part of the cynic's club. No one, and I mean NO ONE, wanted the job of Project From Hell lead. It was a nightmare waiting to happen. And what if layoffs were a reality? Wouldn't it be the ultimate humiliation to be the person who led the effort to transfer knowledge to an outsourcing company that eventually put you out of a job? You couldn't pay me enough to take on that role. And, yet, there it was, and it hadn't come with a raise.

Four jobs in four weeks. And so began the really messy journey leading me to November and bacon.

Chapter Three

The Bacon Grease Gets Hot

I love thee on burgers and salads so green;
On top or on bottom or somewhere between;

Mickey Rives in reply to Darrin Potter: Anyone want to get a petition going? I'm a runner, and, darn it, I like my bacon!

NOVEMBER 8 AT 1:05 P.M.

LIKED BY CAROL BURNS AND TAMARA BRYAN

India Slate in reply to Beth Anne Campbell: Banning an entire food group (yes, bacon is its own food group) is insulting and offensive and just plain unfair. Maybe we need a lawyer to represent us and our rights? ;-)

NOVEMBER 8 AT 1:13 P.M.

LIKED BY BETH ANNE CAMPBELL AND CAROL BURNS.

Beth Anne Campbell in reply to Darrin Potter: BRING BACK THE PIG! BRING BACK THE PIG!

NOVEMBER 8 AT 1:27 P.M.

LIKED BY CAROL BURNS AND CHRISTY DUMAS

Yeah, I was up for a protest. I had a lot of things to protest about, and not just cookies and pork. I am NOT a runner, but, dammit, I like my bacon too! Beyond greasy, salty pork bits, I wanted to protest the outsourcing initiative, because I didn't believe for a second it would work, at least not how it was currently planned. Nor did I believe management when they told us they were doing it for our own good, to free us up so we could do projects. I wanted to protest being stuck in the middle of the Project From Hell, leading the effort to transition our stuff to strangers when I didn't think it could be done at all, let alone in mere months. I wanted to protest the company we hired to do our work because on the first day they showed up, at a meet and greet, their project leaders lined up, and there were 25 men and one woman. I wanted to protest my ungodly schedule and the impossible task of fully engaging in this project while still having a team to manage.

And I wasn't the only one in the mood for revolution.

Sharon Emerson in reply to Darrin Potter: I'm located at the west office. Is this what we have to look forward to???

NOVEMBER 8 AT 1:42 P.M.
LIKED BY CAROL BURNS

Meg Mansfield in reply to Darrin Potter: Is anyone else shocked by the new prices in the corporate cafeteria? I'll be bringing my lunch more often.

NOVEMBER 8 AT 2:12 P.M.
LIKED BY JANET HOLMES AND CAROL BURNS

George Samson in reply to Darrin Potter: Slippery Slope ...

NOVEMBER 8 AT 2:18 P.M.
LIKED BY DONNA PILKERTON AND CAROL BURNS

Beth Anne Campbell in reply to George Samson: That's just a bit o' bacon grease, George ...

NOVEMBER 8 AT 2:29 P.M.
LIKED BY GEORGE SAMSON, ALICE COOKER, ANNE NEWHART, AND CAROL BURNS

Beth Anne Campbell in reply to Darrin Potter: Sharene just gave me a recipe for a homemade cheese ball ... COVERED IN BACON BITS! I slobbered a little when she was describing it ... [no shame].

NOVEMBER 8 AT 4:27 P.M.
LIKED BY CAROL BURNS AND KIM HITCHENS

Christy Dumas in reply to Beth Anne Campbell: I just slobbered a little reading "cheese ball covered in bacon bits."

NOVEMBER 8 AT 4:35 P.M. FROM IPAD
LIKED BY BETH ANNE CAMPBELL AND CAROL BURNS

For some, it was, is, and will always be about bacon. There is no subtext, no metaphor for corporate woes. It's just about the pig. Also, Carol Burns "likes" a lot of things. The "like" function is a great tool, but with great power comes great responsibility. It's like using sticky notes. A few of them are great for reminders, but, when you start having dozens posted around your desk, they lose their influence. People who "like" everything become powerless and also quite annoying. Unless, of course, all the things a person "likes" are worthy of liking. And in this case, I must agree with Carol's overuse of "like." It is justified.

Eve Westman in reply to Darrin Potter: I also enjoy bacon bits on cheese balls and in my salads. Also, I enjoy non-diet soft drinks. Whether or not certain foods and beverages are or are not good for us is a matter of opinion. There are pros and cons of each (from the experts). My opinion: eat/drink what you want but not in excess.

NOVEMBER 9 AT 7:36 A.M.
LIKED BY BETH ANNE CAMPBELL, CAROL BURNS, DONNA PILKERTON,
AND TWO OTHERS

Oh yeah, Eve. Tell it like it is!

Alice Cooker in reply to Darrin Potter: I miss pizza. I'm guessing we'll never get pizza with bacon on it, then …

NOVEMBER 9 AT 8:19 A.M.

LIKED BY BETH ANNE CAMPBELL, JANET HOLMES, KYLE ANDERSON, AND CAROL BURNS

Really, cafeteria pizza? Would it really be that bad to NOT have it on the menu, avec or sans bacon? But, then again, to Alice's point, ANY pizza, anywhere, can be vastly improved by adding real crumbled bacon bits. Pepperoni and bacon? Superb. Supreme with extra bacon? Supremely tasty. Veggie pizza with pineapple and bacon? Too easy, next? Bacon pizza with bacon? *Please, sir … may I have some more?*

Mike Wilkins in reply to Darrin Potter: I see a black market for bacon.

NOVEMBER 9 AT 9:42 A.M.

LIKED BY CAROL BURNS

Beth Anne Campbell in reply to Darrin Potter: This could get ugly … but, if it does, we can all just indulge in some thick-sliced apple-wood-smoked bacon and all will be well with the world.

NOVEMBER 9 AT 9:48 A.M.

LIKED BY CAROL BURNS

I'm sure I could have sold slabs of deep-fried bacon for $5 a slice at this point. And I think the wisdom I presented—that everything in our hearts and souls is better with bacon—is fairly solid. For example, as I write this chapter, I am sitting in my dining room office with my air conditioner set at "South Pole" and a fan pointed directly on me. In the ungodly heat and humidity of the central-southeast USA, it is the only way to keep sweat from dripping down my back and into my butt crack. As a chunky north-erner, I abhor the heat/humidity combo and am subconsciously cursing both my husband Sean for getting a job down here and myself for loving him and moving to this godforsaken kiln with him. Yes, I hate hot and hu-mid with a passion: shorts sticking to thighs, makeup impossible to maintain, no amount of industrial-strength antiperspirant able to block the pits from dripping, mood plummeting, and every move is a sweaty, soppy mess of futile effort. And, yet, hand me a plate of crisp, melt-in-your-mouth bacon strips, and I am Maria Von Trapp at the top of a cool, verdant hill singing "The hills are alive … with the sound of muuuuusiiiiic … "

But wait. Now our story is about to get interesting. We are about to jump the shark. Fonzie just put on his Daisy Dukes, and Richie is revving up the speedboat engine. Yes, they are going to do it.

> **Janet Holmes in reply to Darrin Potter:** What I don't understand is why diet pop is considered "healthier." Artificial sweeteners are definitely not healthy. You're probably better off drinking the non-diet variety if you're going to drink sodas at all.
>
> NOVEMBER 9 AT 9:52 A.M.
> LIKED BY BETH ANNE CAMPBELL, JUAN GRABARRA, KASHA FINN, AND TWO OTHERS

> **Tamara Bryan in reply to Darrin Potter:** I am all for healthy "choices"—emphasis on "CHOICES"—but we have ZERO CHOICES now. You can't even get a packet of freaking MAYO … NO mayo. "Not healthy," was the response when I asked. AND … they raised the prices on ALL the food. Here's to my Charlie Brown Lunch pail!
>
> NOVEMBER 9 AT 9:55 A.M.
> LIKED BY JANET HOLMES, JUAN GRABARRA, AND CAROL BURNS

I'll get to the real crux of the issue in a moment. But, for now, YOU GO, WOMEN! One of the most frustrating things about this type of health mandate is the concept of "healthy." It is a very subjective term. For example, here is Beth Anne Campbell's version of a good health mandate: offer food that is hormone-free, antibiotic-free, pesticide-free, herbicide-free, minimally processed, and grown or raised locally and humanely, such as organically grown fruits and vegetables and meat from animals that eat plants … and charge more for everything else. I just found it ridiculous that the price of a Diet Coke was lower than regular Coke because artificial sweeteners are *so much healthier* than high-fructose corn syrup, right? Pick your poison, people. Actually, sodas in general should all be priced higher because my dentist—let's call him Dr. ~~Hunk~~ Smith—told me soda is the worst thing for your teeth. Even diet soda is bad because acid is acid. OK, to be fair, it was my hygienist Jenny who told me. She usually gives me the best advice because I only see Dr. ~~Dreamy~~ Smith for a few minutes per visit, which is just long enough for a ~~fantasy~~ consult. Dr. Smith did tell me once that genetics and your saliva's pH balance play a big part in dental health, so, in other words, you either have it or you don't. I dated a guy once who ate the worst foods ever, total junk food addict, didn't floss, and had not one single cavity. So he obviously *had it.*

Wow, went way down the rabbit hole there. Also, just to be clear—in case anyone was confused—non-alcoholic carbonated beverages are actually called "pop." Out of respect for 85 percent of the United States of America and greater planet earth, I have referred to it as "soda pop." But please know its proper name.

> **Beth Anne Campbell in reply to Janet Holmes:** Good point, Janet. Therein lies the madness of arbitrary terms like "healthy." There is research out there suggesting artificial sweeteners interfere with the endocrine system (Jillian Michaels has a great book on this: *Master Your Metabolism*). Low-fat food is often heavily laden with sugar and salt to make it taste good. Caffeine is good, caffeine is bad … eggs are bad, no, wait, eggs are OK. That being said … I believe ALL experts agree bacon is a necessary nutrient for all meat-eaters and, as Bart pointed out, a tried-and-true method for choking down hard, bitter vegetables (which are probably heavily dosed with pesticides, anyway).
>
> NOVEMBER 9, 2011 AT 10:04 A.M.
> LIKED BY JANET HOLMES AND CAROL BURNS

Sometimes I amaze even myself.

So now let's get to the grass-fed meat of what's really going on here. Are you ready for it? This is the secret of *Where the Hell Is My Bacon?* So, get out your highlighter.

It wasn't really about bacon.

What? Did I just say that? When is ANYTHING not about bacon??? Shut your mouth! BRING BACK THE PIG! No, I am serious here, folks. It wasn't. About. Bacon. It wasn't really about having to pay $0.50 more for a slice of real cheddar. It wasn't about choking down raw spinach without pork bits or settling for a turkey on marbled rye with fake mayo (or, as I like to call it, *fayo*). It wasn't about the bacon. It was about people feeling like yet another change was handed down with executive dictatorship ... a change they didn't want, didn't ask for, one made without their input, and they were just tired of it. Have you ever heard of employee engagement? You know, when people like their jobs, feel fulfilled and challenged in a healthy way, and are treated with respect, so they just naturally go the extra mile? We had zero. We had the opposite of employee engagement. We had employee repulsion. Utter despair.

The people commenting on the bacon post were just like me. For the first time in years, maybe decades, they hated their job. They had no career satisfaction. Their roles were unfamiliar and unwanted, they felt ignored, and their expertise was not valued. They were overwhelmed, in the dark, and lacked any connection with upper management whatsoever. And they were afraid. Most of them felt they couldn't express their concerns about the direction of the department—like, the outsourcing, too much work, too many people coming in from the outside and not connecting, management not listening, etc. Or, if they did say something, it was ignored or they were told to get on board or shut up. The poor, the hungry, the tired IT professionals did not have a voice. So, they latched onto the health mandate and raised their fists via an innocent pork product. Bacon became the voice of the people.

Looking back, I couldn't be prouder.

> **Christy Dumas in reply to Darrin Potter:** Maybe we should start a fund to purchase bacon or bacon bits to keep in the fridge in the break room. We could run it like the coffee club. Put out a collection box and charge a certain amount per tablespoon of bacon bits?
>
> NOVEMBER 9 AT 10:07 A.M.
> LIKED BY BETH ANNE CAMPBELL, ALICE COOKER, JANET HOLMES, AND
> TWO OTHERS

> **Beth Anne Campbell in reply to Christy Dumas:** I'll bet we could get more than the $0.35 they charge for a cup of coffee … easy.
>
> NOVEMBER 9 AT 10:09 A.M.
> LIKED BY CAROL BURNS

On second thought, running this like the coffee club would not have been a good idea at all. About every six months, our administrative assistant Gena had to send an email nasty-gram to the entire floor threatening to shut off the java flow because there were so many deadbeat drinkers who couldn't pony up a quarter and a dime for a cup o' joe. I personally stopped drinking the coffee from the fourth-floor coffee club even though the alternative from the coffee bar in the cafeteria was five times the price. Why? Because the coffee club coffee gives me diarrhea. I know what you are thinking. Coffee is coffee. But I am telling you there is a difference. My husband Sean used to mock me about this until he started having his own intestinal distress after he bought some Mexican blend K-cups. Suddenly, every day, a couple hours after his first caffeine rush, he was in the men's room dealing with what could only be described as a civil war battle (his words, not mine). Any other coffee brand or flavor or type was not a problem. It was just the Mexican blowing up in his gut. Me, I can drink the Mexican just fine, and my shits are as perfect as a vegetarian's. But the stuff in the coffee club? Mud butt.

Julie Linder in reply to Darrin Potter: This is GREAT ... I love these Yammer comments ... LOL. Made my day a lot better. I thought it was just me with the high prices and the quality of the food. It's terrible.

NOVEMBER 9 AT 10:15 A.M.

LIKED BY BETH ANNE CAMPBELL, JANET HOLMES, DONNA PILKERTON, AND CAROL BURNS

Beth Anne Campbell in reply to Darrin Potter: Sorry, Darrin ... I'm not really trying to start a riot based on your Yammer post, but people like their bacon (and mayo and cheese).

NOVEMBER 9 AT 10:16 A.M.

LIKED BY GEORGE CRIBBAGE AND CAROL BURNS

So, we've seen the anger starting to come out, people getting upset at yet another change made without their input or knowledge. Now you are also seeing the start of a powerful employee engagement experience. Employee engagement was a hot topic in our department at the time. I'm not sure which moron decided to open a very ill-timed survey on the subject right around the time we started to outsource, but you can imagine the results were about as positive as removing bacon bits from the salad bar. I think I can sum up the dozens of questions and their results accurately with this statement: *we hate our jobs, we hate management, and the department has been flushed down the shitter like coffee-club diarrhea.* Our CIO Maya tried to address this in her "I don't really understand you" kind of way by scheduling a department picnic and by forming an innovation team that no one had time to participate in. I mean, the picnic was fine and all, but it was clear she and upper management had no freaking clue what employee engagement really meant or why her department was causing the polar opposite.

But bacon knew. Bacon knows all.

Chapter Four

No One Will Be Laid Off

I love thee on pancakes with syrup on top;
I melt at your sizzle, your sweet, fatty "pop!"

"No one will be laid off."

This was the mantra we heard over and over from Maya and the management team as people continued to express frustration over the changes being implemented. *No one would be laid off.* Why even say it? People start hearing "layoff" in their head like an overplayed '80s song they can't get rid of. Sometimes, when that happens to me, I try to sing another overplayed '80s song to replace the one stuck in my head. If I can't think of one, I do a Google search for "'80s music greatest hits" and play the first one that pops up. Problem solved It's a great trick. You're welcome. But it didn't work with the angry masses. What song replaces "Don't worry; you won't get laid off?" No song is the correct answer. We heard it so much we wondered why they were trying so hard to convince us.

The goal of EGCI was to turn over daily operational support of our systems to an outsourced, mostly offshore team ~~to slash costs via cheap labor~~ ... er, rather, to "allow the employees more time to focus on projects and other important non-support work" (which was another thing they kept repeating as if to convince not only us but themselves). I can't recall one person at my management level or lower on the org chart who really embraced this. Aside from it sounding suspicious, you have to remember this all took place when outsourcing of entire departments was just starting to get really big in our industry. It seemed like every other company was turning over work to offshore teams that came at a far cheaper rate than permanent employees or onshore consultants. A lot of corporations were going this route, both for mass overhauls like ours as well as short-term project-based work. And it wasn't always working out well. Rick Higgins, the software account manager who witnessed my fourth job change during our innovation trip to California, did not have good feedback for us on outsourcing. He worked with dozens of companies across the country comparable to ours in size and industry, so he had a unique insight into the inner workings of similar IT departments. He had only seen one case where the company outsourced only part of their work like we were doing. In many cases, success was lacking. In fact, he had a couple examples where the outsourcing efforts were now being reversed because they had been such colossal failures.

I'm not suggesting outsourcing doesn't work; I'm only reporting what was happening at the time in my limited world. Don't kill the messenger. If you feel yourself getting defensive, go have a few slices of bacon and return to this chapter after you've calmed down a bit over crackly, fatty pork.

To be perfectly honest, outsourcing itself wasn't the root cause of the problem. I liked and respected a lot of the leads that ended up remaining on-site after the transition. They became good friends, and I still keep in touch with many of them even though I have moved on to other opportunities. The company had used offshore development teams a number of times on projects in the past, and it had worked out quite well. And the truth was, we absolutely *were* overworked and in need of some relief. Projects were multi-year and almost always fraught with issues. In my decade as an IT manager and delivery lead, I can't even remember a project that ever went exactly as planned (i.e., on time, on budget, and with no issues). Before, during, and after the EGCI effort, it felt like projects were suspended in a state of continual escalation.

So, yes. The goal for the outsourcing effort (at least, the one they kept telling us) was sound, on some level. It wasn't that we weren't burned out, exhausted, and under enormous pressure to keep the day-to-day going while at the same time working on huge projects. But, like those huge projects—where we were often appealing to management to listen to us—the outsourcing effort was also planned with very little, if any, input from the people who built and maintained the castle halls and knew them better than anyone else.

"No one will be laid off."

When you are trying to convince fearful people that they will still have jobs when all of this is over, you probably shouldn't mandate they take a company-sponsored workshop called "Own Your Career!"— where, among other things, you learn how to update your résumé. I kid you not. Most, if not the entire department got invited to these on-site courses. The material itself was actually pretty cool, and I would recommend this kind of coaching to anyone who is seriously looking to make a job or career change. But to sponsor this type of workshop right in the middle of an outsourcing project when employees were at the height of uncertainty and had been *very* verbal about their fear of job loss? Again, corporate geniuses, take heed: timing is everything. My faith in the executive "Brain Trust" plummeted lower than the Mariana Trench when I tried, in vain, to comprehend how they could possibly think a mandatory workshop on updating our résumés would be taken any other way than "we're preparing you because you might need this soon." Seriously?

This might have been my worst moment during those Dark Ages, sitting in the conference room listening to someone tell us how to organize our work experience and education for résumé optimization. Meanwhile, the stress levels around me were tangible. I might have actually muttered aloud, "Are you fucking kidding me?" But, probably, I just thought it silently, because the instructor was super nice. It wasn't her fault; this is just what she did for a living. But, for us, it was a clear message—and contrary to what Corporate had been repeating since day one.

"No one will be laid off."

The fantastic alternative to "layoffs" was to reassign people to different areas of the department or company. Some of them had worked decades on their current team, in their current role. Imagine being someone who has worked your job (and worked it well) for decades. You've evolved over time, learned new things, and now you're comfortable. Maybe even close to retiring but not quite there yet. BOOM. Suddenly, your entire role is being replaced by an offshore team, and you have no fucking idea what you will be doing, let alone with whom or where. It would be understandable for you to not believe the mantra "No one will lose their job." You are probably really, really scared. The economy isn't great, and you don't even know what is out there. Your kids are in high school or college, and you have cars, houses, and pork products to pay for. Now all of your future is at risk. For all you know, your world might be about to end.

OK, yes, it happens. In this day and age, no one can be complacent about their job, even in one of the few large companies where people expect to work for decades and then retire. But their jobs weren't going away. They were being handed over to strangers—strangers who hadn't created and raised these systems like they were their own children. We were, on some level, the mothers and fathers to our technology. On top of the fear for our paychecks, there was a sense of loss. As much as you sometimes want to put your toddler outside and lock the door after you step on yet another goddamn LEGO during another goddamn tantrum, you still love her dearly because she's a part of you. And, if someone else even joked about putting her outside and locking the door, you'd punch them in the throat.

I couldn't even put myself in the same category of dread as many of my coworkers. I was 11 years into the company, less like a parent to these systems than a crazy aunt who wears purple leggings, earrings the size of corncobs, and too much cheap perfume. There is nothing wrong with that (OK, maybe the cheap perfume). But I wasn't going anywhere. Well, other than my musical chairs responsibility hell, but I was still reporting to the same boss supporting generally the same systems as I had for the past decade. My sense of "am I losing my job?" wasn't quite as high on the scale of the "are you shitting me?" meter as others. Being a lead on the Project From Hell, I was privy to more information than most. Being a manager, I was expected to show support for the initiative, which I truly attempted to do short of not engaging in a social media rant against the removal of bacon bits from the salad bar. I do have my limits.

But even I recognized that voices were not being heard. The cry of the people was ignored. I almost spit out my cocoa-enhanced coffee when I heard we were expected to hand over support for these large, integrated, very complicated systems in a matter of a few months. HA HA HA HA HAAAA! SURELY, you JEST! It took us *six years* to build this system and another three years to stabilize it, but HEY! I'm sure someone can figure it out over the holidays!

In addition to concerns about our ability to transfer decades of knowledge in a few weeks and our "managed sourcing" team's ability to absorb it in a productive way, there was also a lot of fear that the level of support we had been able to give our business partners would shrink like my wardrobe after the holidays. And it did. Flash-forward a few years, and we were still struggling. Eventually, it evened out a bit, but those were some huge rocks to climb, and it was never, in my opinion, nearly as good as it could have been. Or was.

Like the systems themselves, the relationships had been cultivated over time, and you don't just re-create them in a heartbeat. Most of us had worked on some rough projects together with our business partners over the years. It got ugly at times. When you literally work together in the same room for months and months, through Mount Everest-sized successes and black-hole failures, you come to an understanding. Even the worst of your dickhead coworkers becomes tolerable when you've been to the proverbial whipping shed together. And the best of them become true allies.

Maya came on board just a few years after we had completed a major transformation of our Customer, Work Management, Human Resources, Finance, and Supply Chain systems. This massive Overhaul Project had been over three years in the making, with dozens and dozens of systems and software applications being replaced. People were putting in 12-, 14-, 16-hour days for months at a time, and weekends as a rule. Ask Mr. Campbell how many nights I came home and cried—bawled my ass off, heaving and sobbing, ugly-face cried. It was horrible. My stress level was through the roof, and I started wearing a bite guard to alleviate the daily headaches I got from clenching my teeth. I had several knockdown dragged-out fights with consultants and even my own coworkers. Heated discussions were almost a daily occurrence. If ever there were a true "Project From Hell," this had been it.

And, yet, I would go back and do the Overhaul Project all over again in a heartbeat.

It's amazing how much shit people will tolerate when they are well-informed by people they know and trust and who are neck-deep in it just like they are. The technology and business teams had been through many of these battles, and it was hard to imagine not working together in the same way anymore. The Overhaul Project was in many ways much, much worse than the EGCI. But we had been on a mission together, all of us. We were in it as a team. We would win or we would lose, but we would do it as a cohesive, collaborative, supportive unit. People *volunteered* for the Overhaul Project. I begged shamelessly to be included in the effort. Communication was transparent even before the project started, and it came from trusted management staff at every level, all the way to the president of the company. It was clear to all of us that this was important. We didn't hire a bunch of new managers and executives from a completely unrelated industry and start blindly making changes in a way that was foreign to our work culture. Our leaders then were known and trusted, and, subsequently, we wanted to be involved. They didn't make us feel like chattel, and we knew our thoughts and opinions and fears were heard.

My coworkers and I held an enormous and intimate amount of pride in the work we did every single day. Most of us liked being able to build things from the ground up and provide great technical service to our business counterparts. We had relationships that were like second families. We laughed, we cried, we confided in each other. There were many nights over the years when we shared our hopes and dreams and sometimes our nightmares over a beer and pizza. We fought and then forgot we fought. And, sometimes, we'd make our little sister or brother cry, and then blockade the door when they tried to go tell Mom. But, when it seemed as if anyone was being treated unjustly, you better believe the whole family came out with virtual fists clenched.

And, boy, those fists were clenched … right around a handful of salty bacon strips.

Chapter Five

Bring Back the Bacon

I love thee at breakfast or supper or lunch;
Or covered with chocolate for a sugary punch;

Russ Guest in reply to Darrin Potter: My team has officially boycotted the corporate cafeteria. Good news for all the downtown restaurants.

NOVEMBER 9 AT 10:26 A.M.FROM IPHONE
LIKED BY CAROL BURNS AND JANET HOLMES

Jim McHenry in reply to Darrin Potter: No more cafeteria for me. They want to charge $1 for a slice of cheese or $1 for mayo on a sandwich. Ugh! Is it technically a sandwich without mayo and cheese???

NOVEMBER 9 AT 10:26 A.M.
LIKED BY JANET HOLMES, JUAN GRABARRA, AND CAROL BURNS

I think Russ' statement must have made an impact, because, in the years since the "Great Bacon Protest," many restaurants have popped up in the downtown area surrounding the company headquarters. Is it because people stopped eating at the cafeteria during the bacon crisis? Probably. I mean, what is there that isn't somehow affected by the presence or absence of bacon? Months later, after things died down and people weren't waking up screaming in the middle of the night because there was no bacon on the salad bar, and the health mandate had died down, the crowds did return to the cafeteria when something good was served. Like on Stir Fry Day or Build Your Own Pasta Day (unless they only had tofu, in which case it was barren). But the boycotting temporarily did get a lot of people out of the building even in cold November. And, once people start getting away from their desk for a much-needed break instead of blindly inhaling processed food and answering emails, they realize how much better they feel. Studies have been done on this. Google it.

There were not many restaurant selections then, mind you. But there were some. The situation was improving from a few years back when the company first moved downtown. I grew up in the area, and, back in the day, heading downtown was a treat. My grandma used to take us to Marshall Field's, which was like going to a rich people store when you're a child in the '70s, living out in the country sheltered by cows, corn, and freedom. But most of the stores had closed down in the '80s, and downtown was basically a shithole for quite some time. In the early 2000s, the company built their new headquarters there, and now it's actually not a bad place to hang out—still a bit dodgy on the outskirts, but I would expect as much from a city mostly known for its prison and potholes (talking to you, city council).

The new headquarters helped, of that I am certain. But things really springboarded during the "Bacon Era." You're welcome, downtown merchants.

Christy Dumas in reply to Darrin Potter: We could even cook bacon in the microwave if we wanted! Of course, then we would all smell like bacon. Maybe that, in a way, is another form of protest.

NOVEMBER 9, 2011 AT 10:27 A.M.
LIKED BY CAROL BURNS

Beth Anne Campbell in reply to Christy Dumas: You say it like it's a bad thing to smell like bacon.

NOVEMBER 9 10:27 A.M.
LIKED BY CAROL BURNS

Christy Dumas in reply to Beth Anne Campbell: I would rather smell like bacon any day of the week than smell like I took a bath in White Diamonds eau de parfum.

NOVEMBER 9 10:29 A.M.

LIKED BY CAROL BURNS

Beth Anne Campbell in reply to Christy Dumas: Don't even go there ... that's a whole other Yammer conversation. Too soon.

NOVEMBER 9 AT 10:29 A.M.

LIKED BY CAROL BURNS

Smelling like bacon is not a bad thing. Who hasn't awakened one weekend morning and smelled the glorious *odeur de porc sizzlette* and immediately smiled at the thought of a huge plate of bacon waiting for them downstairs in the kitchen?

What is not a good scent is when someone marinates in their cologne or perfume and then brings their cloud of stink into a shared space. Even when it's a good scent like Burberry or Dolce & Gabbana Light Blue, it radiates throughout the office like an atomic odor bomb. And it's never a *good* scent. People who wear Chanel usually know how to take it back a notch. They understand that one should spray the air in front of them and then walk into it. A dab here, a dab there, a little goes a long way. The "marinaters," however, are usually sporting knockoff Fabergé Brut or some Avon crap that hit its peak in the mid-1970s (*Timeless*, my ass). There was such a person in our department who liked to swim in their scent. As with many other inappropriate topics, this social contract violation was aired out—figuratively, not literally—on the Yammer social media platform. Scent Violator was more of a legend to me; I did not know her personally. But, being a hardcore Yammer user at the time, I had of course made some general comments about violating the cologne code of ethics when one of The Marinater's colleagues chose to bitch about it publicly. The Marinater's boss then ripped me a new one, because, apparently, this had escalated into quite an ordeal and the Yammer comments had "not helped." I'm not sure why I got singled out, but, apparently, managers are held to a higher standard.

At any rate, we all know a single pan of fried bacon can kill any bad smell for days, so lessons learned, coworkers of The Marinater. Next time, instead of bitching on social media, get creative.

> **India Slate in reply to Darrin Potter:** Just had to jump in on the bacony goodness conversation ... So, they took bacon away, but they didn't remove regular coffee or energy drinks? I think this is pork discrimination, and we definitely should be protesting the injustice!! BRING BACK THE PIG!!
>
> NOVEMBER 9 AT 10:36 A.M.
> LIKED BY BETH ANNE CAMPBELL, TONIA JACKSON, JULIE LEAVES, AND CAROL BURNS

> **Christy Dumas in reply to Darrin Potter:** We should start a group for this cause. Here are a few ideas and acronyms: People for the Ethical Eating of Bacon in the Cafeteria (or PEEBIC), Company Employees for Bacon (or CEB), or, my personal favorite, Bring Bacon Back to the Cafeteria (or BBB), also known as Triple B.
>
> NOVEMBER 9 AT 10:37 A.M.
> LIKED BY BETH ANNE CAMPBELL, GEORGE CRIBBAGE, AND CAROL BURNS

> **Beth Anne Campbell in reply to Christy Dumas:** BBB—I am adding the acronym to my email signature.
>
> NOVEMBER 9 AT 10:39 A.M.
> LIKED BY GEORGE CRIBBAGE AND CAROL BURNS

> **India Slate in reply to Darrin Potter:** BBB! I'm in. Changing my signature line now ...
>
> NOVEMBER 9 AT 10:40 A.M.
> LIKED BY BETH ANNE CAMPBELL AND CAROL BURNS.

Beth Anne Campbell in reply to Darrin Potter: Looks nice:

Beth Anne Campbell

Mobile, Integration, & System Support

555-555-5555 (Office)

555-555-5555 (Mobile)

BBB!

NOVEMBER 9 AT 10:44 A.M.

LIKED BY GEORGE SAMSON, CAROL BURNS, AND JANET HOLMES

B. B. B.

These initials will now live in infamy.

Bring Back Bacon became the war cry of the department, even the company. If Sally Field had played us in a movie back in the '70s, she would have stood on a table and held up a sign reading "BRING BACK BACON" as she rallied the tired and overworked masses in revolt against such great oppression. If there were a wall between Bacon Germany and No Bacon Germany, Ronald Reagan would have cried "Mr. Gorbachev, tear down this wall and BRING BACK BACON!" If Britney Spears' hair were bacon, the internet would have been crushed with posts of "BRING BACK BACON!" when she shaved her head in a moment of weakness.

I could go on, but that's a lot of looking up things on Wikipedia for the young'uns.

Shari Digger in reply to Darrin Potter: Eating healthy is just one part of it. Without exercise, food alone won't solve the underlying issues of being "unhealthy." If my BMI is under 30, why shouldn't I get to eat what I want?

NOVEMBER 9 AT 10:52 A.M.

LIKED BY CAROL BURNS, MICKEY RIVES, JANET HOLMES, AND

KARL GREEN

Angie Shaker in reply to Darrin Potter: YESSS!!! I'm getting sick of having this healthy eating thing shoved down my throat ... My doctor told me I need to GAIN 25 lbs. and said I should eat Big Macs as often as I want. They should just offer both healthy and less than healthy options and let the person choose!!

NOVEMBER 9 AT 10:56 A.M.

LIKED BY CAROL BURNS AND JANET HOLMES

Tamara Bryan in reply to Sheri Digger: Exercise ... Have you seen our workout room? We have two elliptical machines and three treadmills for 1,500 +/– employees? Really?

NOVEMBER 9 AT 11:23 P.M.

LIKED BY BETH ANNE CAMPBELL, MEG MANSFIELD, AND CAROL BURNS

The masses were angry and getting bolder in their public expression of their frustration. BBB was resonating, not just in IT but in the entire company. When Angie says she's sick of having this "healthy eating thing" shoved down her throat, she doesn't just mean "healthy eating." She means the people at the top of the food chain sucking all of the marrow out of the bones and forcing the bottom feeders to eat the grizzle.

I do take issue with a few points here, though. My BMI is officially "Orca," and I should also be able to eat what I want. We've already established that bacon is the gateway to salad consumption. I'm supposed to eat salad, right? And Angie, dear girl, if your doctor is encouraging you to eat Big Macs, then might I suggest another physician? Wait. You know what? I just looked this up. Big Mac ingredients are not half bad. Not as bad as I thought. I figured they'd be two-thirds soybean, like the "burgers" we had back in junior high in the cafeteria. Yeah, we knew they were made from soybeans; it wasn't a big secret. It's not like you could hide the fact they barely contained actual beef. But they were still super tasty, probably due to all the salt and "natural" flavoring. I mean, the pizza was glistening with pools of oil, too, yet, on Pizza Day, even the poorest of us managed to come up with a couple of bucks for a hot meal. Soy burger and gravy over flaked mashed potatoes? Thank you very much, I'll have two, please. And yes ...

even based on what I thought was in a Big Mac, I still occasionally make a stop at Mickey D's, usually when I'm on the road and there isn't a Wendy's or Burger King in sight. I'm simply saying what I would do and what one's primary physician should recommend are two entirely different things.

George Samson in reply to Darrin Potter: This might be the longest thread on the company's Yammer history ... and it's about bacon. Like times infinity.

NOVEMBER 9 11:31 A.M.

LIKED BY BETH ANNE CAMPBELL, CAROL BURNS, CASSIE TAMARACK, AND FOUR OTHERS

Christopher Willis in reply to George Samson: I was thinking the same thing, but this one has a bit more to go.

NOVEMBER 9 AT 11:40 A.M.

LIKED BY CAROL BURNS

Beth Anne Campbell in reply to Darrin Potter: This thread is popular because those of us under the "carnivore" umbrella have an inherent, physiological need for bacon. This is a fact-like statement backed by anecdotal science. I think the popularity also underscores the need for some occasional levity in our social media environment. (By the way, thank you, coffee bar, for putting out some of those delightful scrump-dillyicious cookies ... riot averted).

NOVEMBER 9 AT 11:52 A.M.

LIKED BY JERYL LAMPMAN AND CAROL BURNS

I felt the need to defend our honor. This string of comments did go on to officially become the longest thread in the company's Yammer network. I feel like we should have a big trophy, in the shape of a pig.

Do we really physiologically, biologically need bacon?

I tried to Google it to find some proof, but I mistyped "psychological" instead of "physiological" and kept getting links to material on Francis Bacon. While I bow to Francis Bacon not only for his amazingly fortuitous name but also his contribution to the scientific method, this was not helpful in my research. So I will resort to basic logic. Does bacon make us feel good? Yes! Is feeling good healthy? Yes again! If we don't feel good, will our health deteriorate? Indeed. Therefore, notwithstanding, nevertheless, I conclude we have a physiological need for bacon. Our bodies WANT to be happy, therefore healthy, therefore to eat more bacon.

Rob Maschevitz in reply to Darrin Potter: Speaking of Bacon ... I deep fry 8–10 pounds of thick-sliced bacon every couple months. Store it in a re-sealable bag in the refrigerator. This lasts me almost two weeks. Remember, pork is the other white meat, and we need bacon to survive.

NOVEMBER 9 AT 11:56 A.M.

LIKED BY BETH ANNE CAMPBELL, CHRISTY DUMAS, KIM HITCHENS, AND TWO OTHERS

Beth Anne Campbell in reply to Rob Maschevitz: During my lunch break today, I am going to construct an altar to Rob Maschevitz. I have tasted his deep-fried bacon. I think I actually had an out-of-body experience.

NOVEMBER 9 AT 11:58 A.M.

LIKED BY LIZ ALEXANDER AND CAROL BURNS.

Rob Maschevitz in reply to Beth Anne Campbell: Deep-fried bacon is excellent. I also use pork for making homemade kielbasa ... I use bacon as the fat content in the recipe.

NOVEMBER 9 AT 12:01 P.M.

LIKED BY BETH ANNE CAMPBELL AND CAROL BURNS.

I know to some of you this may sound odd. Deep-fried bacon? Because bacon generates so much fat itself, it may seem strange that one would further fry it in oil. With traditional bacon-frying, aren't we already sort of deep-frying it? Unless, of course, you are using a microwave … and let me just say, I would NEVER judge anyone for utilizing a microwave to cook bacon. The mere act of cooking bacon exempts you from any scorn you might get from so-called bacon snobs. I'm not saying the microwave is my number one choice for preparing those little slices of pork heaven, but I am privileged to have a large cast-iron skillet and time, so I tend to go old school on my bacon methodology. For those of you using a microwave, bless you for engaging in the bacon experience, despite your limited means.

And the answer is no. Fried bacon—as in, fried in a pan or in the oven—is NOT exactly the same as deep-fried bacon. Rob brought in some of his deep-fried bacon once. I thought I was waking up from The Matrix. Imagine your best slice of bacon ever. Maybe it was your first, when you were but a bacon virgin. Maybe you lost your *birginity* after the age of three and therefore actually remember the experience—which is both *fortunate,* for you have this most precious of memories, and *unfortunate,* because you could have been eating bacon for a good two plus years previously and missed out. Maybe it was that time your brother took you to this cluttered little BBQ joint in northern Indiana where you consumed some downright magical pork belly and thought you might spontaneously combust with pure joy. Perhaps it was being the first person down at the orange kitchen counter back in '78 when Mom had just put the pile of bacon on the table and none of your six siblings were up yet. Whatever it was, all of us bacon lovers have a Peter Pan memory of eating this delicacy. Your eyes roll back into your head when you put a slice of really, *really* good fried pork into your mouth. Imagine this moment … and then increase the elation exponentially, and there you will have deep-fried bacon.

The first thing that hits you is the amazing bacon flavor. Like no other cut of animal protein, the flavor in a deep-fried bacon slice is enhanced immensely. Think of a cheap, store-bought birthday cake—whipped, tasteless frosting, dry cake, way too sweet (if that is even possible)—compared to homemade cake with buttercream frosting, made with freshly churned butter, cream, eggs just pulled from the henhouse, and real vanilla beans just shipped in from Madagascar. This is the difference between traditional fried bacon and deep-fried bacon. NOT that I am comparing traditional bacon with store-bought birthday cake. I simply used the example as an illustration of the difference in flavor.

Actually, a more accurate comparison would be the best pizza you ever had in your life (traditional bacon), and then the best pizza you ever had in your life at your favorite vacation spot on the most perfect day ever with your dream dinner guests (deep-fried bacon). Which, for me, would be Klavon's pizza (Jackson, MI), in Hawaii (Maui), on the beach at sunset, with Kelly Clarkson, Chrissy Tiegen, Jada Pinkett-Smith, Michelle Obama, Gal Gadot, and Emily Blunt. Slumber Party in Lahaina (bacon on the pizza, of course).

After the flavor hits you, the bacon starts to melt—literally melt—in your mouth. You barely have to chew deep-fried bacon. You do not have to try and generate saliva; trust me, it will be on overdrive. You might start to go through the motions. Your mouth might start moving up and down, tricked by all those other times you ate bacon and had to chew it. Even if it was cooked perfectly, you still had to give it a good chew. But, now, your teeth barely have to move. There is a slight crunch, and then, like Elvin magic, the bacon-y goodness is released onto your tongue.

> **Beth Anne Campbell in reply to Darrin Potter:** OMG! As I was writing my last comment, an ANGEL OF BACON stopped by and delivered two boxes of BACON POPCORN! I kid you not! The fourth floor WILL smell like bacon this afternoon. When you all get a whiff, holler me a "BRING BACK BACON" so the world will understand our solidarity in pork ...
>
> NOVEMBER 9 AT 12:03 P.M.
> LIKED BY ROB MASCHEVITZ, KASHA FINN, DARRIN POTTER, AND CAROL BURNS.

WHAT?! I get BACON GIFTS?! What have I done to deserve this???

Christy Dumas in reply to Beth Anne Campbell: Me = Jealous!!! Are you sharing the bacon popcorn???

NOVEMBER 9 AT 12:03 P.M.
LIKED BY CAROL BURNS

Beth Anne Campbell in reply to Christy Dumas: Of course not. Just kidding ... I will share with bacon lovers far and wide. The only thing better than consuming bacon or bacon-flavored food products is consuming them with a fellow or sister bacon fanatic.

NOVEMBER 9 AT 12:13 P.M.
LIKED BY CAROL BURNS AND LIZ ALEXANDER

Beth Anne Campbell in reply to Darrin Potter: FYI, I have received a couple of offerings of bacon items thus far, so I have erected a Bacon Shrine outside my cubicle. Please feel free to stop by and oink so the bacon gods will bless you.

NOVEMBER 10, 2011 AT 4:21 P.M.
LIKED BY MICKEY RIVES AND MEG MANSFIELD

I actually did not share any bacon popcorn with Christy, and I hope she forgives me. But, in reality, this seemingly wondrous gift actually tasted like a dirty grill, and I threw it away. It did make the fourth floor smell like the inside of a pig smoker, though. If you are so inclined to delve into bacon popcorn, I might suggest a high-end gourmet brand, or, better yet, make your own. Unless, of course, you like the taste of a dirty grill, in which case, have at it and enjoy!

P.S. Anyone who would like to offer me gifts ... deep-fried bacon would be a great option.

Mickey Rives in reply to Beth Anne Campbell: It's official, *BBB* is going into the company acronym list now ... should be there by tomorrow!

NOVEMBER 9 AT 12:38 P.M.
LIKED BY BETH ANNE CAMPBELL AND CAROL BURNS

BBB was officially placed in the company acronym list. I wonder if it's still there. If not, I hope the person who removed it is cursed by having savory bacon strips just out of reach for the rest of their life. I hope they are served the most amazing BLT in a restaurant, but then there is a fire, the sprinklers go off, and the sandwich falls to the wet floor in a soggy mess. Or maybe they are on a beach holding the last piece of bacon from the picnic basket when a seagull dives down and snatches *The Precious* out of their hand. Perhaps they come downstairs on a Saturday morning and find their six siblings have eaten all of the bacon and there isn't any more and they live 30 minutes from the nearest grocery store.

By the way, best BLT I ever had was at Zingerman's Deli in Ann Arbor, Michigan. On Challah with a potato latke on the side. It was not soggy at all.

Tamara Bryan in reply to Beth Anne Campbell: MAYO ... MAYO ... MAYO ...

NOVEMBER 9 AT 12:58 P.M.
LIKED BY CAROL BURNS

You heard correctly. Mayo packets disappeared from the cafeteria just about the same time bacon bits did. Coincidence? I THINK NOT.

Beth Anne Campbell in reply to Tamara Bryan: Tamara, I don't know what this means (maybe some subversive movement growing in the company underground), but I just had a lunch meeting catered by the cafeteria, and there were ample packets of ... wait for it ... MAYO ... pro-vided. Also, there was real provolone cheese and some really delicious cookies. I looked around for a camera, because I thought I might be on "Punked" or "Candid Camera." If there was one, it was well hidden. But, as you may have expected ... no bacon. :-(

NOVEMBER 9 AT 1:28 P.M.
LIKED BY CAROL BURNS AND ANNE NEWHART

Like the bigger corporate picture at the time, the mayonnaise conundrum only added to the frustration. They took away something. But then it showed up elsewhere. There was no consistency. If mayo is bad enough to remove from the cafeteria, then why not remove it from the catering as well? It was the same with the outsourcing rhetoric. You SAY I'm not going to lose my job, but you lie about other things, so why should I believe you? It's not hard to see how this whole bacon thing got under people's skin. And it goes without saying: when your company has new executive management, strangers are being hired in left and right, you are outsourcing, and, at the very least, faced with the prospect of a totally different job than you've had for 20 years … taking away comfort food is probably not the best idea.

Why am I not an executive? I often ask myself this. I haven't quite figured it out yet. Probably one reason is that being a manager is not my favorite role, not by a long shot. I also swear a lot. I don't have a pedigree (MBA, PhD), and I barely know how to speak "business." I can't kiss ass. I know some C-levels who have overcome all of these stereotypes and more, yet still the status quo seems to dominate. Or it could be I'm just not smart enough to run a company but smart enough to know I'm not smart enough to run a company. Or something like that.

> **Thomas Jackson in reply to Darrin Potter:** A "like" in this thread means you like bacon, right? I don't want this misinterpreted as "I like the fact that bacon was removed from the menu."
>
> NOVEMBER 9 AT 1:34 P.M.
> LIKED BY CAROL BURNS

> **Beth Anne Campbell in reply to Thomas Jackson:** Yes, Tom. If you "like" any comment in this thread, it means you are in the I Love Bacon club (a.k.a. BBB).
>
> NOVEMBER 9 AT 1:49 P.M.
> LIKED BY CAROL BURNS

Jon Sprocket in reply to Darrin Potter: There is a great routine from Jim Gaffigan regarding this exact topic.

NOVEMBER 9 AT 1:55 P.M.

LIKED BY CAROL BURNS

Do yourself a favor and Google "Jim Gaffigan Bacon." Jim and I are kindred spirits in the bacon world. While every carnivore has some grasp on fried pork, Jim really understands bacon at the soul-level. He's also funny all around, so do yourself a bigger favor and get one of his books or watch one of his comedy specials.

While eating bacon, of course.

Chapter Six

Chaos Builds

I love thee in muffins or big cheesy balls;
I love thee when pan-fried, grease spattered on walls;

The "Managed Sourcing" project, a.k.a. Project From Hell, a.k.a. Employee Growth & Contracting Initiative or EGCI, was in full swing when the bacon tragedy occurred. We've already discussed what a miracle it was that people were even talking about bacon, because the post almost didn't happen, and it almost didn't happen because we were up to our ears in the transition of a decade of knowledge. Weeks upon weeks of sitting in rooms with our dozens and dozens of experts painstakingly reviewing every nook and cranny of the systems they had built from scratch like a homemade maple-bacon muffin. There were so many knowledge transfer sessions going on at once that we had to rent rooms in the building across the street to accommodate all of them. Those were followed by reviews, then more transition, then updates, then more reviews, then assessments and scoring.

And this was on the heels of two months in the underworld of getting it all ready.

As it became clear we were absolutely moving forward with outsourcing, the panic started to bubble up. Those of us deeply engulfed in the actual transition process had less time to think about it, but also those of us whose day job it was to manage people heard about it every hour of every day. As soon as we were official, in late summer, the bubbling panic came to full boil. I could have cooked linguini in the panic.

As we moved closer to the reality of managed sourcing, the leaders of this undertaking revealed we were going to do this in three months. In one quarter of one year, we would transfer all knowledge of our world to a group of strangers. This may seem like a lot of time to the average person. In reality, it was absolute insanity. I thought it was a joke when they announced this; I seriously thought they were kidding. Anyone who knew anything about our systems should have known better.

One large piece of our technical suite was a robust mobile application I knew very intimately. This was an app used by thousands of field technicians to manage and complete their work. A dozen or so of my coworkers and I had built and rebuilt it several times over half a decade. It had just gone through an extensive transformation as part of the aforementioned Overhaul Project. It took almost three years just to get it put into production, let alone stabilized. I knew personally how complex it was, because I was one of the technical leads for the communication part of this application on the Overhaul Project. As part of my involvement, I had completed over 40 lengthy design specifications over hundreds of hours. I remember when the expert consultant told me he thought I could complete one of the bigger design specs in 30 minutes, maybe an hour tops. I nearly shit my pants right there in the conference room and that would have been embarrassing because my mom wasn't there to do my laundry. I countered his 30 minutes with 120 HOURS for one design, no joke. And guess who was right? THANK YOU! Three solid weeks of full-time work just to complete one of 40 designs, which wasn't even half of the entirety of the design work for the overall application. That was how complicated this one application was (and there were dozens more just like it). Even three years after the Overhaul Project ended, we were still uncovering bugs and tweaking performance. It was hell when we built it and only a little less hell maintaining it. And we did all of this already coming to the table with several years' experience working on an earlier version of the same mobile application before the big Overhaul Project even began.

To say we were skeptical in believing an inexperienced team could become experts in *three months* would be the understatement of the year. We were baffled.

We hadn't even gotten over the idea of turning over our technology children to strangers when we got wind of the detailed schedule. This one mobile system's team of over a dozen experts would be sitting in a conference room for only about a month, rehashing every nuance of this huge beast. After the knowledge transition part, there would be a few weeks of job shadowing (where the outsourcing team would look over our shoulders as we did work), a few weeks of "reverse" job shadowing (we look over theirs), and then it would be done. The systems would be 100 percent in the hands of the new team, including handling middle-of-the-night crisis calls trying to figure out why shit wasn't working and all hell breaking loose. Three months start to finish. Piece of cake. Hand me the specs for the Space Shuttle; I got this.

And then there were the resource gaps in the outsourcing team. We were days from kicking this thing off and hadn't yet identified anyone who had at least a little (or any) experience in several of our more critical applications. There were painfully few experts in Work and Asset Management back then. In other areas like Human Resources, they had a larger and better pool to pick from. HR was a little more established and stable. Work and Asset Management was booming, and technology was still very much in a growth stage. Expertise simply hadn't caught up yet.

Before we could begin transitioning, we had to interview and select some really good leaders from the outsourcing team. Those folks would remain onsite and manage the offshore team as well as transition the knowledge he/she/they received to any new resources who came on board later. So, it was critically important to have someone in the lead position who was not only experienced in the software we were using but also a good manager, coordinator, and quick learner.

One of our biggest and most important systems managed customer outages. For this software we could not find anyone with even moderate expertise. So, we settled for "good manager/coordinator and quick learner," which was still a struggle. It's not that there weren't capable people; there absolutely were. But the magnitude of the system and the expectation of support seemed to frighten people off. Over the course of several weeks, we interviewed and selected three different leads, all of whom "coincidentally" left the assignment within days due to "family emergencies." It really was a borderline ridiculous coincidence, assuming it *was* a coincidence. I'm not saying they all didn't have true family emergencies. I'm just saying, if I had a dollar for every time someone's grandparent or mother wasn't doing well over the course of the outsourcing project, I could buy you dinner at Red Lobster.

The "sick relative" excuses came so often it became a joke, but, in fairness, I've experienced far worse. Like Lou from the Overhaul Project a few years earlier who had "lobster poisoning" one week and then "food poisoning" a week later. Lou had at least three delayed or cancelled flights on Mondays from airports in popular vacation destinations. He was young and single, and, apparently, he liked to travel and mingle. And then there was Car-crash Rhonda, the consultant project manager who couldn't make it to work due to her car accident but then posted about a party she was going to on Facebook. She was a hot mess. I've experienced a few colorful stories from company employees too. All I am saying is, consultants are the masters of excuses, and I say this as a consultant.

The three leads who all had sick family members and quit were illustrative of the glaring lack of expertise for some of our major systems. I honestly don't blame them even if they were just making shit up. It was a daunting job, and even someone with a long history of using or supporting the software might have had reservations. Coming in blind would have put my stomach in knots. In the end, we decided to not turn over support of that particular system to the outsourcing team. Good move.

Then there was the scheduling of the individual sessions themselves. What a great time that was! All of the experts of these to-be-transferred systems—the ones who built them, maintained them, knew them inside and out—had to attend weeks of workshops. They had to dig out and provide all documentation. They had to help organize and prioritize the workshop material. Then they sat in dim, windowless rooms with a bunch of strangers and painstakingly went over every detail of their systems while the outsourcing team took copious notes. Each week on Friday, there were review sessions, where the outsourcing team presented back to us what they learned to make sure they absorbed everything. These were called "Playback Sessions." If they successfully received, processed, and documented the material, then we would move on. If not, we revisited the missed items and tried again. Then the whole cycle began again with the next piece of the system. It was an immense amount of work for both the company people and the outsourcing team.

And, while all of this was taking place, the company experts still had to run, fix, maintain, and update their systems and continue working on projects in full flight. If we asked management what the top priority was—and we did—the answer we often got was "Everything is a priority." We had to find a way to do it all.

It's not hard to see why morale was in a sinkhole and the air of resistance was brewing in the clouds. So, of course, what better way to help people to understand and to reassure them than to remove the most precious of all things from the cafeteria salad bar.

Chapter Seven

We're not Going to Take It

I love thee on pizza that's piled up with cheese;
I love thee on 'taters, with sour cream, please;

Tamara Bryan in response to Darrin Potter: I was at the Northwest plant today, and I forgot my lunch. So, I decided to get a salad in their cafeteria (I thought it would be a safe choice). Guess what? **They have bacon bits there.** BUT ... they are pre-packaged into very small containers and you have to pay an extra $0.50 for them. Same for the shredded cheese, which is also pre-packaged for you at the fee of $0.50. I guess we can't be trusted with choosing our own quantity of toppings either ... at least, not the ones they deem "unhealthy." Apparently, you can have as much brown broccoli or dry carrots as you want, no extra charge. Also, buyers beware ... they are now making you weigh your dressings along with your salad. In all seriousness, are they trying to price themselves out of business? I picked up some comment cards. I'm not sure they'll do any good.

NOVEMBER 10 AT 1:34 P.M.
LIKED BY LESLIE COLEMAN BARD AND TRENT PARKS

Bacon bits were available in some of the other facilities (outside of our corporate headquarters) but at a premium. And, if I may be so bold, in quantities no self-respecting bacon eater would tolerate. It was an insulting amount, maybe a tablespoon or two maximum. While, yes, any amount of bacon is good, this meager portion would barely begin to register in a cheap cafeteria salad where it has to compete with such yucks as kale, whole chickpeas (why?), and dry, borderline expired turkey. That's like putting a single slice of bacon on your BLT. NOT EVEN CLOSE, Northwest Plant Cafeteria!

Elena Schemp in reply to Tamara Bryan: I brought my own bottle of Thousand Island today. At least if I have to pay for my dressing on my HEALTHY lunch, I will have the dressing I enjoy! If I now have to pay for cheese too, well I guess I'll just start bringing my own salads, or go to Derek's Cafe where I can get an awesome salad for $5 with free rolls! THEY don't weigh my dressing.

NOVEMBER 10 AT 1:55 P.M.
LIKED BY JANET HOMES AND JASON GOODY

Mickey Rives in reply to Tamara Bryan: "Bring Bacon Back" bringing bacon back, but beware big-ass bucks. Bummer, bank broke.

NOVEMBER 10 AT 2:14 P.M.
LIKED BY TIMOTHY BEAN

Oh, Mickey, your alliterations blow my mind! Mickey was right. The situation was getting out of hand. You don't appease those who are already in career turmoil and about to engage in major edibles upheaval by raising the price on EVERYTHING that tastes good. Remember the French Revolution from history class? The insurgents were on the verge of storming the bacon Bastille.

Amelia Warren in reply to Darrin Potter: The bacon and mayo have both now been kidnapped from the Dunning Street Cafeteria. Shedding a tear ...

NOVEMBER 10 AT 2:46 P.M.
LIKED BY ALICE COOKER AND JANET HOLMES

Kasha Finn in reply to Darrin Potter: What's left? Are they still selling chips, bagels, muffins, cookies, etc.??? Anything?

NOVEMBER 10 AT 2:59 P.M.
LIKED BY BETH ANNE CAMPBELL, ELLEN O'ROURKE, AND CAROL BURNS

Sharon Emerson in reply to Darrin Potter: Oh no! I have been in Portland all week. Oh well, I will just have to bring in my own mayo when I get back.

NOVEMBER 10 AT 3:08 P.M.
LIKED BY JEN PARKER

Damn. Spoke too soon. They are already storming.

But this brings up another good point. This was a corporate edict. If this health initiative was so important, why wasn't it communicated clearly and consistently, company-wide? Crazy. (I have some alliteration skills, too). Some places lost bacon bits altogether (RIP). Some had it but charged more. This is like when my parents renovated our attic, adding three bedrooms. The oldest, my brother Joe, got his own room. Steve, who is younger than me, got his own room. Me, the second oldest, HAD TO SHARE WITH MY SISTER! WTF, Mom??? How is that fair? Fortunately, my brothers both got into trouble and had to move in together, freeing up Steve's room for my sister Sue and allowing me to have my own room, finally. Of course, it took several years. No one was going to wait years for bacon.

Jen Parker in reply to Tamara Bryan: I have started bringing my own cheese and raisins and almonds and REAL ranch dressing from home. As long as I'm still keeping track of it in my food log, who cares? I like flavor on my salads. Like Bart said, that's how we eat tasteless vegetables.

NOVEMBER 10 AT 3:15 P.M.
LIKED BY BART SWARTOUT, CHRIS MILFORD, AND DAN STARK

Jeryl Lampman in reply to Tamara Bryan: OK, here's the thing. I just recently visited the cafeteria at the local hospital. Guess what! They serve pizza, burgers, French fries, salads ... and also the healthy Salad bar lets you can make your OWN FREAKING CHOICES for what you want. You want fat-free dressing? Regular? No problem. IT'S A HOSPITAL. Where you go to get healthy. Are we, like, Kindergarteners? We know what is healthy for us. We are not idiots. We should have the flexibility to make those choices. I feel sorry for the people at the cafeteria cash register. It is clear they are getting surprised with the new changes that seem to come in every day. Corporate is treating everyone like "Fast Food Hostages." Where is Liam Neeson when you need him???

NOVEMBER 10 AT 3:32 P.M.

LIKED BY WILL VANDERMEER AND TRENT PARKS

Jason Goody in reply to Tamara Bryan: Jeryl, YESSS! I was just thinking the same thing. I could see more people starting to leave for lunch instead of staying internal, which sucks with winter approaching.

NOVEMBER 11 AT 9:13 A.M.

LIKED BY JANET HOLMES

Rene Glass in reply to Tamara Bryan: Judging by the overflowing trashcans in the parking garages, everyone is eating out already!

NOVEMBER 11 AT 9:54 A.M.

LIKED BY ELLEN O'ROURKE

Lena Hirsch in reply to Tamara Bryan: This is all great information—thank you so much everyone! I can tell you for certain I won't be going to the cafeteria anymore. This is ludicrous.

NOVEMBER 11 AT 10:06 A.M.

LIKED BY JANET HOLMES

Jaden Frank in reply to Tamara Bryan: Naomi Stephanelli told me she ordered a Reuben, and they told her they weren't allowed to use Thousand Island dressing anymore. How do you make a Reuben without Thousand Island dressing?!?!? THIS IS ANARCHY!

NOVEMBER 11 AT 10:21 A.M.

LIKED BY JERYL LAMPMAN, ELLEN O'ROURKE, AND THREE OTHERS

In defense, many dictionary sources (among them Merriam-Webster and dictionary.com) define a Reuben as "a grilled sandwich of corned beef, swiss cheese, and sauerkraut usually on rye bread." No dressing mentioned. But, also, in defense, Wikipedia defines it as having "Russian dressing," which is kinda-sorta like Thousand Island dressing but spicier and not as sweet. But since no one in my world really knows what Russian dressing is, and this is the Midwest where we like what we like, we opt for Thousand Island. Frankly speaking, a Reuben needs some sweet in there to counter the tang of the sauerkraut and the saltiness of the corned beef. Actually, I'm more of a Monte Cristo person, but that's another story. Regardless of whether the classic Reuben has dressing or not, the point is … WTF? It's a *schmear* of dressing on a sandwich. Hardly the worst offender in the sandwich yet ripped from under Naomi like her confidence in her job.

Beth Anne Campbell in reply to Darrin Potter Look, I'm not going to knock the Cafeteria as an industry. I have had some mighty tasty things down there (herb-crusted pork loin … *mmmm*). I just agree with Darrin and many others that we should Bring Back the Bacon. And Mayo. And real cheese made with real cow's milk. :-)

NOVEMBER 11 AT 11:11 A.M.

LIKED BY GEORGE CRIBBAGE AND CAROL BURNS

Shana Fontain in reply to Darrin Potter: As criminal as our executives want to make bacon out to be, apparently they are anti-cheese, too! I was salivating while reading comments about bacon cheese balls, and cheese & bacon bits on salads, (yum!) but now, if you want cheese on your sandwich, it's an extra $1, and something you should "eat in moderation!" Great way to push business out to the local restaurants. No doubt more people will be heading out for lunch now.

NOVEMBER 11 AT 11:16 A.M.
LIKED BY CAROL BURNS

We've already discussed how illogical it is for things that inherently and descriptively contain cheese to be cheapened by removing cheese. They don't become less expensive and healthier; they become nonexistent. A grilled cheese sandwich without cheese is just toast. Or maybe a simple bacon sandwich, because why have grilled cheese without bacon? In any case, without cheese, a grilled cheese sandwich is not a grilled cheese sandwich. You can't say, "I'm going to charge you extra for cheese on your grilled cheese sandwich." You can charge me extra for cheese on my sandwich. You can charge me extra for cheese on my toast. But you cannot say, "If you want cheese on your mac & cheese, you have to pay more." NO! If I refuse to "pay more" for cheese on my mac & cheese, it's NOT MAC & CHEESE! It's just MAC!

I also contend it's not really cheese if it's not made (at least mostly) from actual milk from an actual animal. I mean, kudos to all of y'all vegans out there but it's a sacrilege to call something "vegan cheese." At least have the respect to add "Product" to the end of it. "Vegan Cheese *Product*" is at least in the realm of honorable. Look, I applaud your lifestyle. It is clearly superior to us carnivores (at least, that's what I'm told often by my vegan and vegetarian friends). Admittedly, for as much faith as I put into bacon, I know it won't extend my life an extra 20 years like your fiber-rich, über-vitamin macronutrient diet will. But, in the interest of making you meat haters feel like you're a part of the evolutionary club, we've tainted the good name of real, milk-based cheese by including it on any product one might sprinkle on top of macaroni. I know this will elicit all kinds of hate mail. Bring it on. I'll counter your negative energy with some authentic aged white cheddar and tasty Gruyère cuddled up against a stack of thick-sliced applewood-smoked bacon nestled between two slices of fresh sourdough bread that have been generously slathered with real cream-based butter. Your negative review will quickly disappear from my mind like cheesy bacon dip at an office holiday party.

It wasn't really the cafeteria's fault. And they did make a mean herb-crusted pork loin.

> **Benny Little in reply to Darrin Potter:** Congratulations! This thread is now the longest in Yammer history.
>
> NOVEMBER 11 AT 12:07 P.M.
> LIKED BY CAROL BURNS, CASSIE TAMARACK, MICKEY RIVES, AND TWO OTHERS

> **Beth Anne Campbell in reply to Benny Little:** We haven't even gotten started yet.
>
> NOVEMBER 11 AT 1:09 P.M.
> LIKED BY CAROL BURNS

> **Anne Newhart in reply to Darrin Potter:** This Yammer rant is long, in part, because our dear Beth Anne Campbell is back!!!!! We've missed you, Beth!
>
> NOVEMBER 11 AT 1:47 P.M.
> LIKED BY BETH ANNE CAMPBELL, CAROL BURNS, AND ALICE COOKER

Anne is one of my favorite people ever. There are few people in this world whom I would let drag my inflexible ass to a yoga class at lunch hour, and she is one of them. I am humbled by her comment, and I include it here to illustrate how long it had been since I had been able to engage in the Yammer phenomenon. Anne is happy to have me back because she, like many others, was sick and tired of the YAAAWN posts of late. Just because it's a platform used by a business doesn't mean it always has to be business material. The same applies with work in general. Shame on those who still advocate maintaining a distance from their coworkers or team members. I'm not saying let them read your Laura Palmer diary. But Jesus, Mary, and Joseph … you spend time with people for *eight hours a day!* Or more! That's one-third of your weekday life; why wouldn't you want to have a little fun with them? They are your WORK FAMILY! It's OK to talk about your kids or your dogs or your hobbies (unless your hobby is collecting toe jam, in which case, leave that shit at home). Your social media doesn't always have to be about the next generation of your enterprise software or how to be a good leader. Sometimes it's OK to talk about Hallmark Christmas Movies or *World of Warcraft* or a cool leather bag you found at the flea market. Post a cat picture every so often! It's OK! Your work family will love you even more.

> **Anne Newhart in reply to Darrin Potter:** Also, if people are going out for lunch, I believe Rocky Top has a burger with battered deep-fried bacon. Yes, you read correctly. BATTERED, DEEP-FRIED BACON. Which I personally have not tried, but I've seen it. I had to do a double take, because I wasn't sure it was actually real.
>
> NOVEMBER 11 AT 1:48 P.M.
> LIKED BY BETH ANNE CAMPBELL, CAROL BURNS, AND CHRISTY DUMAS

> **Beth Anne Campbell in reply to Anne Newhart:** LIKE TO THE *N*TH POWER!
>
> NOVEMBER 11 AT 2:00 P.M.
> LIKED BY ANNE NEWHART AND CAROL BURNS

> **Darrin Potter in reply to Anne Newhart:** I heard about that burger! Massive. I am going to have to try one soon :-)
>
> NOVEMBER 11 AT 2:28 P.M.
> LIKED BY ANNE NEWHART AND CAROL BURNS

I cannot continue with this tale without addressing the Rocky Top burger mentioned by Anne. I no longer live where the Rocky Top Beer-BBQ & Grill resides, and, although I much prefer winters in my new southern-ish residence, I cannot deny the burger selection in my new city pales in comparison with the Rocky Top burger menu. The Billy Burger is the one Anne is referring to: "grilled and seasoned burger topped with our signature beer battered bacon on a toasted brioche bun." Why ... don't mind if I do! Or maybe the Mac Bacon, with house-smoked mac & cheese and smoked bacon. I'm sorry, is that my drool on the page? My apologies. I doubt anyone would want to substitute the Black Bean Burger for the real meat version—but know it is available—and also, if you did that, you would be dead to me.

Christy Dumas in reply to Darrin Potter: After all this bacon discussion yesterday, I felt compelled to have bacon last night for dinner. Nothing is better than breakfast for dinner!

NOVEMBER 11 AT 2:35 A.M.

LIKED BY BETH ANNE CAMPBELL, LENA HIRSCH, AND CAROL BURNS

Breakfast for dinner is never a wrong thing, especially when it contains copious amounts of fried pork. I'm not sure who ever decided that bacon and cheese omelets were only appropriate for the morning meal, or pancakes with bacon and maple syrup did not make the "Sunday Dinner" list. Fortunately, many churches, VFW Halls, and other rebels around the world have violated this unwritten rule. This has increased the popularity of eggs, bacon, and waffles at any meal, resulting in the availability of the 24-hour breakfast—thank you Denny's and other fine food chains. Now if y'all could just work on crisping up your bacon a bit. Don't get me wrong; there is no bad bacon. But let us make sure we honor the bacon gods adequately by ensuring the 1:30 a.m. Saturday bacon is as crisp and fresh as the 8 o'clock Monday morning bacon. Also, I should be able to actually chew it with human teeth. Franchise sub shops, I'm talking to you. I love ya, but your bacon is always soggy, what up? You can do better; I believe in you. Please and thank you.

Bart Swartout in reply to Darrin Potter: Speaking of unreal burgers, I was in San Antonio, TX, a while back and had the God of all Burgers. It puts all other burgers to shame. Imagine a half-pound of premium Angus hamburger, followed by a half-pound of smoked brisket, topped by five thick applewood-smoked slices of bacon, rounded off by a slathering of barbecue sauce. I nearly passed out while consuming this masterpiece. Every burger I have ordered since pales in comparison.

NOVEMBER 11 AT 2:47 P.M.

LIKED BY BETH ANNE CAMPBELL, LENA HIRSCH, AND CAROL BURNS

With all due respect, Bart … not enough bacon. And thank God he did NOT pass out. Someone might have snatched that masterpiece from right under him. What a crime.

Ryan Fowler in reply to Darrin Potter: Corporate should be ashamed for the extreme financial burden they are placing on my family. If I want to eat myself to an early grave, it should be my choice … but now I'm going broke doing it. :o)

NOVEMBER 14 AT 7:39 A.M.
LIKED BY GEORGE SAMSON, MEG MANSFIELD, AND CAROL BURNS

Rick Mandela in reply to Darrin Potter: I am even more pissed that they have gotten rid of the bacon (or sausage), egg, and cheese bagel for breakfast. Those healthy breakfast burritos are nasty! Evidently, I'm not the only one who thinks so, because I see a lot of leftovers every day. They were my TGIF treat until a few weeks ago.

NOVEMBER 14 AT 8:31 A.M.
LIKED BY CAROL BURNS

Jon Sprocket in reply to Darrin Potter: I am pretty sure they have a comments/suggestion box down at the cafeteria. Just curious if anyone submitted a BBB-related suggestion.

NOVEMBER 4 8:37 P.M. FROM DESKTOP
LIKED BY CAROL BURNS

Lena Hirsch in reply to Darrin Potter: Wait a sec—you have to pay a buck for cheese on your sandwich? Isn't this America????

NOVEMBER 14 AT 9:25 P.M. FROM DESKTOP
LIKED BY BETH ANNE CAMPBELL, CAROL BURNS, JANET HOLMES, AND KARL GREEN

To be fair, and to reiterate, this was not the cafeteria's doing. It came from Corporate. But we were so desperate to release our rage that we weren't thinking straight, and we directed our anger at the closest thing to bacon:

the people who physically put it on the salad bar. But they were innocents caught up in the good—but misguided—intentions of a corporate vice president. Pawns in an ugly game of control. They were probably just as upset as us, because you KNOW food service workers sneak some of the good shit in the back, and who wouldn't nab a finger full of real bacon bits when no one was looking? I used to work for a caterer and HELL YES I grabbed a spoonful of bacon-tater salad from the walk-in fridge on occasion. So, while I am certain people DID put suggestions in *The Box* (as Jon Sprocket—not his real name, but I wish it were my name—suggested), I doubt they had much impact.

I only once ever put a suggestion into *The Box* for the cafeteria: a desperate plea to bring back croissants. They mysteriously disappeared one day like my faith in humanity after every election. There was no warning, and this was not during one of the bi-yearly health kicks such as the one that murdered bacon bits on the salad bar. This was a random event. One day I could order egg salad on a croissant. The next day, my soft, buttery egg salad cradles were gone. I thought, perhaps, it was a fluke—a careless stock person had put them on the wrong shelf. Or maybe in some odd cosmic coincidence—or a crappy entrée selection—an inordinate number of hungry analysts had opted for the sandwich station and used them all up. But the next day was the same. And the next. Week after week, no croissants, until finally I asked. *WHERE THE FUCK ARE THE CROISSANTS???* OK, maybe it was more like the young "sandwichmeister" finally got tired of me asking and volunteered that croissants were no more. I may have frozen right there, unblinking, for about 45 seconds. It was awkward. Finally, I broke out of my shock and pushed my tray on without responding. I had Cheetos for lunch that day, if I recall correctly. With a Diet Coke.

Why people do things like this to their fellow human beings is beyond me. And, in case you are wondering … no, they never came back, at least not while I was there (someone tell me if this has changed; I will start looking at job postings and seriously consider northern winters again). Apparently, croissants do not hold such status in the food world as bacon, because no one protested and there wasn't a Yammer post anywhere to be found. Shame.

And then, a little bit of hope on the bacon front.

Beth Anne Campbell in reply to Darrin Potter: I would like to personally thank the person on the third floor for taking the initiative to try and solve this life-altering problem. I found the attached Change Navigation matrix in the break room. I can't express how much I appreciate your support. It is innovative ideas like "Save money by bringing in your own bacon" that change the world.

NOVEMBER 14 AT 10:56 A.M.

LIKED BY KYLE ANDERSON, SHERYL CLAROLL, GEORGE CRIBBAGE, AND TWO OTHERS

Tool #1 Reflection		
The Change: *Removal of Bacon Bits from the cafeteria*		
	Challenges	**Opportunities**
You, personally	PISSED!!!!! Blame the baboons	Save money bringing in your own bacon
Your Team	*Is very sad ...* ☹	Bacon revolution

Bart Swartout in reply to Darrin Potter: I didn't really embrace this type of change management tool, but, now that I see it used in such a meaningful way, I'm sold. This really underscores how powerful a tool it can be to get though the change. I'm inspired.

NOVEMBER 14 AT 11:04 A.M. FROM IPAD

LIKED BY DARRIN POTTER

Bart Swartout in reply to Darrin Potter: Also, I laughed for a solid two minutes upon seeing this matrix. Thanks for sharing, Beth. And thanks to the genius who created it.

NOVEMBER 14 AT 11:05 A.M. FROM IPAD

LIKED BY GEORGE CRIBBAGE

I found the scribbled Change Matrix on a table in the third-floor break room. I cannot even express how much I worship the individual who put this masterpiece together. The level of sarcasm to which he or she or they sank, and the ingenuity in trying to solve our bacon problem with a change management matrix is … well, it puts a tear in my eye if I'm being truthful. The pain coming through in the oversized *PISSED* sentiment breaks my heart. The tiny words expressing how the team is "sad" reflect how tiny our souls were at the time. And then, just as I am about to start weeping with empathy at the utter despair my coworkers are feeling … as their pain is about to split my heart in two … the opportunity "Save money bringing in your own bacon" spares me from soul death and warms my entire being with love and pride. Even though I know this opportunity is futile, I feel a glimmer of hope where before there was none.

And yes, I DO blame the baboons!

Kevin Weeper in reply to Darrin Potter: A growing trend in urban revitalization is to eliminate the corporate cafeteria entirely and encourage employees to visit local food establishments. Is there anyone around here who has a salad bar? I know Scotty's Ranch does, although it's at the other end of downtown, probably have to drive. Can't think of others. I work at the Portland office, so I don't know the area there. We've got Lucia's across the road from us. They have a salad bar, but, sadly, they don't always have bacon bits, and, when they do, it's the fake kind.

NOVEMBER 14 AT 1:54 P.M.

LIKED BY KARL GREEN AND GEORGE SAMSON

All decent salad bars should have real bacon bits. It should be federal law. I'm not talking about the token salad bar you sometimes see in the corner of the Chinese buffet or the local pizza place, clearly put there for your vegan cousin visiting from Oregon or the one dude who will not deign to put a carb in his body. Frankly speaking, those fake salad bars don't deserve to have fried pork bits in the vicinity. There should not be real bacon bits next to the wilted brown iceberg lettuce and shredded Saharan carrots, because then people would expect quality salad fixin's across the board, which would just complicate things. You can't mix "awesome" with the food equivalent of despair. People would get confused and wonder if they should put on a nice tuxedo jacket over their dirty jean shorts and faded Guns N' Roses tank top or wear Bruno Magli with their pajama sweats instead of flip flops. The dichotomy of real sizzling pork nuggets touching brown, soggy cherry tomatoes would cause a paradox in the universe.

No, I'm talking about real salad bars, where you find whole boiled eggs, 14 varieties of real cheese, pine nuts, and homemade salad dressing next to the arugula. The kind of bar with pasta salad, where you're not really sure the name of that particular pasta (Rigatoni? Penne? Fusilli?), and you can see the bits of Parmigiana-Reggiano cheese clinging to the olive oil-caressed exterior. THAT is the kind of salad bar that by law should require mounds of real bacon bits. If you should encounter this type of real salad bar and find it isn't properly accompanied by real bacon, then you should immediately report the restaurant to the Department of Public Health. If the restaurant managers don't have half enough of a brain to understand the essentials of a good salad bar, then they will surely have at least 32 health code violations. Do you really want to eat at a place where the grill never gets cleaned? Logic.

And if ANY salad bar has something labeled "Bacon Bits" but they are clearly—and I'm getting nauseated even thinking about this … give me a second—if they are clearly *imitation "bacon" bits*, then run. "The Flash" your way out of that joint and make your way to the nearest grocer, where you can buy a pound of commercial-brand bacon. Go home, fry it up, sit in the corner rocking back and forth with a slice of Oscar Mayer in your mouth, and try to forget the horror you just witnessed.

> **Jason Goody in reply to Darrin Potter:** As if things could not get any worse, I just heard they are eliminating the unlimited refill cards on fountain drinks at the Portland cafeteria in a few weeks. NOOOOOOOO!!!!
>
> NOVEMBER 14 1:58 P.M. FROM DESKTOP
> LIKED BY BETH ANNE CAMPBELL AND KEVIN WEEPER

Hey, Corporate, why don't you just take your bacon-greased longsword and shove it further into my soul?

> **Bart Swartout in reply to Darrin Potter: Check out the amazing Bacon Explosion:**
>
> http://www.bbqaddicts.com/recipes/pork/bacon-explosion/
>
> NOVEMBER 14 2:14 P.M. FROM IPAD
> LIKED BY JON SPROCKET

OK. Now we're talking. Shit's about to get real.

Chapter Eight

Failure and Such

In quiches with spinach I love thee as such;

The mass knowledge transition sessions for the EGCI project were themselves transitioning from frustration to raw chaos to numbness and back over again as we spent hours, days, weeks sitting in rooms trying to suck decades of expertise from our team and into the blank slates of the outsourcing team. Additionally, we were dealing with dozens of strangers. The vast majority of them were from India and grew up in a culture very different from our own. Our company was quite diverse, and we were no strangers to people coming in from outside of our smallish midwestern city. But we had little opportunity to meet our new partners and get to know each other on an individual basis before we were put into a room with one another and had to jump right into some intense technical subject matter.

They had mannerisms we didn't understand, and some of their accents were thick. I'm sure some of us were difficult for them to understand as well. There was definitely an "us versus them" undertone, and I'm a little ashamed to say, this was mostly on us. Our outsourcing team was accustomed to going from place to place for this type of transition. They were savvy travelers, living in multiple cultures, and a lot of them were very young. For some of them, this outsourcing work was just a stepping-stone to other things. It made sense that they were probably a little more accepting of change than we were as a whole. We had careers at a company where one could fully expect to work their entire adult life. This was the only real career job many of us had ever had. We were the stable ones, a large family, and you know how it is when one of your siblings brings home a new boyfriend or girlfriend. They have to walk the proverbial gauntlet for a while until you're sure they aren't too clingy or snobby or a major dick.

Eventually, we got some cultural training, which helped immensely, but it was several months into the effort. The speaker for this training was awesome, and he walked us through some things we had noticed but not understood … like head nodding that wasn't really a "yes" or a "no." One of the things the speaker talked about in the training was how failure might be perceived in his culture versus in our Smalltown, USA world. For some of our partners, failure was not an option and was treated very seriously, especially by some of their older team members.

OK, no one really likes failure, but most of us at the company had grown up with what I'll call "Standard Midwestern Values." That is, we know we will fuck up (and often), our parental figures and peers will let us know when we fuck up, and, as we grow into adulthood, we develop an underlying awareness that our failures are more lessons to learn from. They suck, but we know we become more resilient because of them. We are generally a rebellious people and don't listen to good advice, because we are determined to do what we want. It doesn't mean we are bad people or failures at life … just that we fall, skin our knees, then get back up again and shake it off.

Sometimes the straight-A student gets a C– in gym sophomore year of high school, and she joins Band so she doesn't have to go to gym class anymore. Lesson learned. Sometimes, the university kicks you out because of your shitty grades, and you have to sleep on a coworker's couch until you can save up enough money for a cheap studio rental in a dodgy part of town. Then her racist husband kicks you out, because, while they were on vacation, you dared to let your black coworker sit at the dining room table for five minutes *inside the perimeter* while you changed your clothes after work before going out. You realize later, after you are settled into your cheap studio rental in the dodgy part of town, that it will never be as bad as sleeping on a coworker's couch for two weeks and getting kicked out by her racist husband. And you also have learned to not associate with people who would kick you out of their house for having non-white friends. Failure equals lessons and failures make us better people.

The fact that failure was perceived a bit differently by some of our outsourcing team was already old news to me. I had experienced a few incidents. It was very clear to me that anything less than 100 percent success would not be taken well.

The process for transitioning our technical knowledge for this effort involved weekly Friday meetings, during which the outsourcing teams presented what they had learned back to us (the "Playback Sessions"). This was to ensure they had accurately and completely understood and captured what we had covered. At the end of the Friday presentation, we would give a pass or fail to the receiving team. It wasn't even a fail, really. We didn't call it that. It was more like "didn't quite get it, need more work, not quite passing." Very gentle, not like the time a bunch of us failed our algebra tests in seventh grade when Mrs. Casler found cheat notes in some people's desks and flipped out the next day in front of everyone, threatening to fail us all for the entire semester and not just the test. For the record, when someone passed me a note asking for the answer to a question, I wrote, *I don't know* every time even though I did absolutely know, 'cause I ain't no cheater. And no, I did not fail the class. I got an A. I think Mrs. Casler knew.

No, this was not like that at all. We had to make sure the knowledge needed to support these critical systems had been adequately passed on. If it wasn't, then more work was needed. That was as much on us as it was on the receiving team. If we gave out a "needs more work," then we had to try a little harder, too.

But some of our new partners did not look at it the same way.

One Friday afternoon, we were reviewing our big work management mobile application. I happened to be acting as Subject Matter Expert for this extended transition as well as Transition Lead/Coordinator. I attended daily sessions for weeks with the rest of the experts to pass on my knowledge as well as organize and coordinate the meetings. For the first couple of weeks, the reviews went very well. We were at the "basics" level, and they seemed to be picking it up quickly. By the third week, we were getting into some rather heavy technical material. Remember, those of us on the transition team knew this Kraken up and down. We had built this baby from the ground up, some of us having gone through two, three, or even four iterations of previous versions of it for the past decade. We had supported it day after day for years. There were a lot of nuances that were not easy to explain, many of them based on the complexity of the data passed back and forth. Getting to the data was not straightforward, and there was a LOT of data. The work it managed was critical to our customers and critical for the safety of our employees. There was regulation involved. So, given all of this, I was not surprised at all that it started to get a bit tricky to absorb. You don't just sit someone down in a room and talk for a few weeks and then put them in the pilot's seat of a commercial jet. It takes some time, and, in spite of us trying to drill this into the powers that be, our voices of reason had gone unheard. So it was a sprint when it should have been a marathon. There were bound to be some torn hamstrings here and there.

After this particular review, it was clear some important concepts had been missed or misinterpreted. For the company folk, this was no biggie. It was the story of our lives. We poured our hearts and souls into this technology. Then something would break down, we'd sigh, we'd fix it, and we'd make it better. Sometimes, we would get the heat of management or executives or regulators, so we would keep working on it, and all would be good. Repeat infinitely. This was not a failure to us, it was a "take a deep breath, let's try again." But the receiving team took this very differently.

At the end of the session, we gave our feedback. "We made a lot of great progress this past week, but, as expected, things are starting to get complicated. At this time, we think we need to go over some things again before we pass."

There was silence. We were over our time in the conference room and another group was lurking outside. They were giving us the glare of doom.

Respect. I would do the same thing, even if the president of the company was in the room. A reservation is a reservation.

"We'll go over the gap areas next week and try again before we move on. We'll get there. Everyone have a great weekend."

My team had already started to gather up their materials and make for the door. As I stood up to do the same, the outsourcing team lead came over. I could tell he wasn't happy. I looked over at the table where his four team members were still sitting, with their heads down but looking at us out of the corner of their eyes. They didn't seem to be packing up to vacate the room, in stark contrast to the rest of the group.

The team lead stood in front of me. "Beth, what is this; why are you not passing us? This is not right; this is not acceptable!"

Although his voice was low, it was shaking with a sense of authority, and I could tell by his demeanor he was very angry. My team froze in their tracks. A couple of them had the "Oh, shit" look on their faces. I was taken aback a bit. Again, for me, this wasn't a big deal. There were some gaps, and we would figure it out and try again. It was not unlike testing software, an activity I had been heavily involved with over the previous decade. You build a product to the best of your ability and the specifications given. You test it yourself. You think you have gotten every bug out of the thing and are beaming with pride when you hand it over to the people who are most familiar with the process or product, the ones who will be using it. You let them go to town during user testing. And then they find things. Always. It doesn't matter how well you coded or configured or scripted or installed or whatever. They always find things. And then they tell you about them so you can go back and fix the stuff that isn't right. Your ego remains unscathed, because that's how User Acceptance Testing works. It ain't no surprise.

That's all this was: User Acceptance Testing for our knowledge transition sessions. I would have been SHOCKED if we went through multiple Godzilla systems for weeks and didn't have some challenges with the concepts.

But Team Lead did not agree. He was piiiiiiiisssssssed.

"What is it you think we did wrong?"

I probably stood there for a few seconds not speaking, mostly because I honestly did not know how to react. His team members were now fixated on us from their seats around the table. My team was continuing to pack up but in slow motion because this was like a car crash to them. They had to watch. And no one was making a sound except for the oblivious people entering the room for the next meeting.

"Ravi, you didn't do anything wrong. There are some gaps in the playback; we talked about those." I listed a few. "This is normal; it's a big system. We just need to cover a few things in more detail; that's all."

Ravi was not having it. He insisted we not wait until the next Friday but, rather, cover the gap areas earlier in the week and do another review no later than Wednesday. It was clear he took this very personally, and nothing I said would alleviate his concern. I actually felt bad for him. I hoped he wasn't getting some kind of pressure from his management. There is nothing I hate more than bully managers. But, later, when we had our cultural training, they talked about failure. I don't think it was management. I think it was something inherent to how Ravi and some of his colleagues were brought up, with a sense of pride that was in overdrive.

I had to respect that. Any sense of pride in what one does is admirable, even if it goes a bit too far. I have worked with some fine people in my life, people who take ownership of their work as if it were their child. It's a trait far more valuable than anything you can learn from a book or a university. And conversely, I have worked with some people who just go through the motions. They do only as much as needed to get their work done with no sense of honor. They just don't care. I would rather have someone confront me because they cared about their work than for someone to stay silent because they didn't give a shit.

Once we better understood how our new partners thought and worked and spoke and moved, it became much easier for most of us to communicate. They weren't the enemy. They weren't the problem. The problem was the group of people at the top of the company management food chain who continued to display utter lack of understanding of how to relate to the masses below.

I remember at some point during this ordeal recognizing how little connection the new CIO had with the department. She would stand in front of us at town halls, trying to convince us this outsourcing effort was a good thing. It wouldn't have mattered. She could have been telling us we all got 20 percent raises in honor of Thanksgiving, and most of us would have sat there with skeptical looks on our faces. She simply did not have any rapport with the audience. When she told us we were not going to lose our jobs, she said it like it was such a ridiculous thought to even have, as if we were toddlers. Like, *don't be silly.*

Everything that came out of her mouth, or the mouths of her hand-picked (and mostly externally hired) staff, was designed to try and convince us this was for the better. But that's like a creepy stranger trying to convince you to buy artichokes in the grocery store at 3 a.m. You don't really need artichokes, and they aren't on your grocery list. In fact, you've never had one and you think they might be kind of gross. You're a meat and potatoes kind of person. Your staples are ground beef, chuck roast, bacon, of course, and Yukon Golds. They have worked for you for years, and you're relatively healthy. You rarely eat green vegetables unless they are smothered in cheddar and bacon, and the artichoke doesn't look like it would hold cheese very well, just speaking your truth. And, frankly, you're only in the produce section because it's a pass-through to the frozen pizza aisle. But the creepy stranger is insisting you must buy artichokes and eat them. You are crazy if you don't. They clearly know best and are trying to reassure you—in an impatient, semi-patronizing sort of way—that everything will be fine. Because they know better. You won't gag, you won't get sick, and, in the end, you will be grateful you tried them. Your life will be glorious. They don't listen when you say, "I don't understand artichokes, and I don't think that's what I need right now. I'm scared to try them. And you're creeping me out; who talks to total strangers at 3 a.m. in the produce section? No one. Except creepy people."

HELL no.

But, if your best friend forever was shopping with you on a Saturday afternoon, and they told you they had just tried artichokes for the first time and they were AMAZING, absolutely delish with some melted butter and dill, you might pause to consider. You aren't sure, but you are willing to hear more. Your BFF knows you need to eat red meat at every meal because you are anemic (because they are your BFF and they actually attempt to know something about you). So, they suggest that steamed artichokes with melted dill-butter would be incredible with a nice *grass-fed New York Strip Steak*. Medium, of course, because anything more is leather and anything less is raw. They even offer to cook it for you, and now you are stoked, because you know your BFF is a great cook. Suddenly, you are enthusiastic about artichokes. GAME ON! You trust your BFF because they listen to you ... that's why they are your BFF. You know that, no matter what, they got your back. Your BFF was the one who stamped out the fire you drunk-lit at the bus station one late night back in college and didn't give you up when the bus driver called campus police. They didn't think any less of you when you laughed so hard while sledding you peed your pants. Badly. They did not judge when you started crying on a really long, totally uphill hike (OK, road) to the top of Montalto at Monticello ... and, when you insisted they go on without you, they did. Because that's what you wanted, and they trusted you to tell them if you needed them to stay.

We needed a BFF to communicate this shit, but, instead, we had a creepy stranger in the grocery store at 3 a.m.

By the way—and don't take my word, ask your BFF—steamed artichokes are fantastic with melted dill-butter and served with just about any protein, including bacon. I've had some good artichokes and some mediocre artichokes and some "WTF?" artichokes. Not unlike major outsourcing initiatives, the key is to understand how to properly cook and serve them.

Chapter Nine

A Brilliant Idea

And wrapped 'round a shrimp, oh I love thee so much!

Beth Anne Campbell in reply to Darrin Potter: The fourth floor is holding a "BRING BACK THE BACON" Protest Buffet on Friday, November 18. Fellow and Sister Bacon-lovers (or just food lovers), please feel free to contribute and consume via our business center ... or, better yet, organize your own potluck! (Bacon-full AND Bacon-less dishes all accepted; we do not discriminate against vegetarians ... as long as it's in the spirit of bacon, it's acceptable).

NOVEMBER 14 AT 5:43 P.M.

LIKED BY SHANA FONTAINE, WILL VANDERMEER, AND FIVE OTHERS

As the anger around the removal of bacon from the salad bar grew, it became clear we had to take this to the next level. As the self-proclaimed orchestrator (some might say *instigator*) of the Yammer thread, I felt some obligation to bring this whole thing to a climax. I wanted to have, on a grander scale, the same feeling one has as when one bites into a slice of crispy, fatty, thick-sliced bacon for the very first time. I knew this couldn't go on forever, but we had to go out with a bang (or maybe, a POP, like bacon grease sizzling in a cast-iron pan).

One afternoon, I was walking to my next knowledge transition session when it hit me. I was trying to clear my mind of what lay ahead, hoping and praying I wouldn't make one of our partner leads mad again with a "needs more work" grade. I didn't want to think of the massive amount of work coming in the days, weeks, and months ahead. My mind was numb, probably from denial and a subconscious attempt to quell the exploding stress ball brewing in my stomach. And, of course—as eternally—I had bacon on my mind. It was the perfect storm for crazy ideas, and I had one: we needed a bacon potluck.

The idea was perfect on many levels. The obvious one was, what better way to crescendo this thing to the top of Pork Mountain than to have a bacon-themed event? IN YOUR FACE, CORPORATE! I imagined our little fourth-floor breakroom flooded with all kinds of hickory-smoked goodness. It would smell like bacon everywhere. People on the elevator going to the 10th or 12th floors would stick out their heads in childlike wonder when we fourth-floor residents stepped off the lift. We would look back with a knowing smile but say nothing. You take our bacon away? We will bring it back a hundredfold. The message would be loud and clear and savory.

Another justification for a bacon buffet (as if we needed one) was the fact that, just a few days *BB,* Maya announced that our traditional floor-by-floor holiday potlucks were going away. For decades, through multiple corporate headquarter locations, each floor or department of the company had enjoyed a December feast that consisted partly of company-sponsored dishes and mostly of employee potluck contributions. The company would pay for a vat of meatballs or mac & cheese catered from one of our local fan favorites. The masses would contribute such memorable delights as bean dip, chili, cheesy potatoes, breakfast casseroles (with bacon!), and all sorts of sweet concoctions. Several lazy people would bring in a tray of powdered donuts from the gas station or a bag of store-brand chips. One health nut would offer a large vegetable tray, which would still be three-fourths untouched at the end of the day. It was glorious. Each break room was a different food nirvana, and, after our initial feast around 9:30 a.m.— because we really couldn't wait until a proper lunch time—we would all go wandering to different floors to sample their offerings. It was like one big, beautiful continent with all the countries cooperating in food alliance. The small breakroom environment was very intimate, and we got to catch up with our coworkers around the trough. The floor-to-floor crawl allowed us to see people we hadn't talked to in weeks beyond the occasional nod coming into the building at the start of day.

Everyone looked forward to this yearly event. And then it was taken away.

Someone higher up had decided a better option would be to have one big buffet for everyone in the auditorium over a long lunch. Not intimate. Not an all-day event. There would be no wandering back to the breakroom at 2:30 p.m. to grab the last ham and cream cheese pinwheel or to scrape a bit of hardened cheesy hash browns from the bottom of a slow cooker. No sneaking to the buffet at 4:15 p.m. and hoping no one noticed it was, like, your seventh trip since lunch because, damn, those caramel brownies were so freaking good. Nope. None of this would be happening, because the Holiday Potluck just went from "small, intimate gathering" to U2's "Rattle and Hum" concert. If you don't know who U2 is, just insert your mega star football-stadium concert scenario.

There would be food in the auditorium, but it would also be loud. There would be a finite window in which to graze. There would be hunger pangs in the late afternoon and no potluck remnants to quell them. The worst part was the mass of people. I can tell you that, in the several years I attended these auditorium buffets, the lines were very long. And, while the food was tasty, it wasn't quite the same. It's not as easy to have a quick catch-up with someone in a noisy room full of 500 people. Sure, we might run into someone we know, but it's no different than seeing them coming into work: dozens of bodies passing each other. There wasn't anything egregious about the mass-produced potluck; it was just different. And the timing could not have been worse. Just when we were all clinging to any tiny drop of familiarity to our former work lives, and struggling with the change, the executives had yet another brilliant idea to rip the fabric of our souls to shreds. A big buffet is fine—it's like going to a wedding—we've all been there. It was just a shitty time to convert.

But, like many things coming from Corporate, timing is everything. Sometimes it's not what you do but how and when you do it.

I'm not sure why the change from intimate office picnic to the Woodstock version of potlucks came about. Perhaps it was part of the very misguided employee engagement effort that was getting headlines as we ramped up to the "managed sourcing" initiative (because what better time is there to become concerned about employee engagement than when morale and confidence are at their lowest and fear at its highest?). Employee engagement surveys had been sent out with abysmal responses. They responded by giving us access to social media sites previously blocked on our internet. Then another survey came out. Still shitty. So, the department heads and CIO decided to have a couple of picnics. Again, not unlike the mass buffet switch, it wasn't inherently a bad idea. Who doesn't love a picnic? I do! I love picnics! With golf and entertainment, no less! I went to the first picnic, and I enjoyed myself. But I never lost sight of the fact that this really wasn't what employee engagement was all about. And a lot of other people weren't duped, either. Fun, work-sponsored activities are great, but they don't make people feel valued. They don't alleviate fear, and they don't make change easier to manage or understand. When you plan things like picnics or baseball games or an after-dinner gathering at the local pub, they can be wonderful bonding experiences … *if your team is already confident and stable and satisfied*. When you do these things with a department in chaos, smart people see through the superficial motives. We say to ourselves, this is great, but how is this helping us through these uncertain times? Smart people become more skeptical, not more trusting.

The buffet switcharoo was the last straw for me. But, as they say, when someone doesn't buy you flowers, go out and grow your own. So I grew my own.

A couple days after the first Yammer post on the universal ruler, Bacon, I ran into Bart Swartout in the business center. He was getting community coffee from the breakroom. I was holding my real coffee from the coffee bar downstairs, because I didn't bring any *Imodium A-D* with me that day.

Bart and I got to talking. Of course, the topic turned to bacon (as should every topic).

"I think we should have a bacon-themed potluck for the team," I said. "I mean, they took away our holiday buffet. At least, this way, we can have a little of that back. Plus …"—I cocked my head for emphasis—"It's *BACON-themed*."

I knew he had the same thought running through his head: it's for "the people," but, really, the ulterior motive is we, personally, get to eat scrumptious bacon stuff en masse. Bart had already mentioned the Bacon Explosion (Turducken for pork) recipe in the Yammer comments, so I knew he would be on board. I just didn't know how much "on board" he really was.

Bart was staring at me with eyes glazed over like a slice of candied bacon, his cup of coffee suspended in midair as his first sip was halted by an epiphany.

"Oh yes," he began, shaking his head. "Absolutely. Brilliant. But not a *team* potluck. We *need to take this company wide*."

Oh yes indeed, Bart. This is why I like you so much. You. Just. Get it. As my husband often says when I womansplain things to him, "You've crystalized my thoughts perfectly." Bart and I were on the same wavelength … a wavelength that followed the gentle curves of the white lard in a strip of bacon. As I thought about it for a moment, I realized Bart was onto something important. I could not, in all good consciousness, plan a potluck in honor of the most sacred protein on the planet only for one relatively small team. This could not be under the radar. There were hundreds of people in the building, and it would be a sacrilege to make this exclusive. Lack of transparency was one of the things we were frustrated with in our current situation with management. And it wasn't just the IT department dealing with these issues. Our woes were corporate wide. So, therefore, the bacon buffet must be corporate wide.

I didn't have the bandwidth to organize a buffet for each floor and all of our satellite locations, but I did have access to the company-wide email list. And I used it.

****

"BRING BACK THE BACON" BUFFET!

WHEN: *FRIDAY, NOVEMBER 18, 8 a.m. THRU AFTERNOON GRAZING*

WHERE: *FOURTH FLOOR BUSINESS CENTER, CORPORATE HQ*
(and wherever else you want to bring in tasty bacon food)

WHY: *TO ENJOY THE SAVORY GOODNESS OF BACON-INFUSED DISHES*
(and also to enjoy tasty bacon-less dishes)

WHAT DO I HAVE TO DO? *BRING GOOD FOOD!*
ESPECIALLY IF IT CONTAINS BACON!!!

(Or not. Non-bacon dishes are also welcome and encouraged, as a courtesy to our friends who incomprehensibly do not consume bacon. Cheese strongly encouraged.)

IF YOU WOULD LIKE TO PARTICIPATE BUT ARE UNABLE TO COOK A SAVORY BACON-FULL OR BACON-LESS DISH, THEN PLEASE STOP AT WALMART AND PICK UP A BAG OF CHIPS OR SOMETHING. OR BRING SOME POP. SNAG SOME DONUT HOLES. SOMETHING.

(If you can't even find the time to stop at the 7-11 and get a box of Pop-Tarts or some off-brand pork rinds, then please eat in the cafeteria).

This message was posted with full respect for those who do not eat bacon or even meat. We don't get it, but we respect you. Plus, some of your food is most excellent, and we want to eat that, too.

For those of you who have not been in the loop, here is a little background: last week a verbal riot nearly ensued when it was reported on Yammer that the cafeteria had removed bacon bits from the salad bar because they are "unhealthy" (see Yammer for the full thread; it is worth viewing). Whether this mandate came from Corporate or the café itself is irrelevant. It was clear that *the removal of the bacon bits hit many close to home. For some employees (who may not even eat salad!) this perhaps represented a more global state of affairs: **the removal of choice**.*

As one astute Yammerer commented, " ... Without those little bits of paradise we call bacon, I will just head over to Wendy's and get myself a Baconator. Which kind of defeats the purpose of removing bacon bits in the first place."

Well said, my brother in bacon. Well said.

*The **BRING BACK THE BACON BUFFET** is taking place as a light-hearted, informal protest to this decision. Additionally, as most of us are well aware, consuming bacon and other tasty baconless food is a GREAT way to improve employee engagement!*

As a courtesy to our friends and co-workers who do not consume bacon, please label any bacon-less or meatless dishes accordingly. I will be bringing vegetarian sesame noodles—with bacon on the side for those who would like to ... enhance ... the experience ...

****

Game on, my friends. Touchdown with a football made of pigskin from a pig who was sacrificed to the bacon gods. What? A bit much? Perhaps, yes. Sorry vegans and vegetarians; I got carried away. I apologize if I offended anyone. Also, footballs aren't really made from pigskin; they are probably made from leather, which is from a cow, not a pig. Cows are also tasty, but I'm not going to go there. Let's just say the announcement of the "Bring Back Bacon Buffet" ignited a fire in our company ... a hickory-wood fire over which hundreds of bacon slices were sizzling in utter unity.

India Slate in reply to Beth Anne Campbell: When is this amazing event going to take place? I can't wait!

NOVEMBER 15 AT 8:04 A.M.

LIKED BY MISSY KIRKLAND AND CAROL BURNS

Beth Anne Campbell in reply to India Slate: The official date is this Friday, 8 a.m. through whenever. The fourth floor is coordinating one effort. Anyone contributing to the fourth-floor BBB buffet/potluck is welcome to also consume. If a given floor finds they have enough participation; they should consider hoarding all of their bacon-full and bacon-less dishes in their own business center.

BRING BACK THE BACON BUFFET

NOVEMBER 15 AT 8:12 A.M.
LIKED BY JEN PARKER, CHRISTY DUMAS, AND FOUR OTHERS

Naomi Bronkowski in reply to Beth Anne Campbell: I am IN LIKE FLYNN! Been wanting to try out some bacon recipes; now is my chance. And for a good cause. Look out bacon; here I come!

NOVEMBER 15 AT 8:43 A.M.
LIKED BY JANET HOLMES AND CAROL BURNS

Missy Kirkland in reply to Bart Swartout: I had the once-in-a-lifetime opportunity to indulge in the Bacon Explosion when a friend made it last year. It might just be the most amazing thing I have ever put in my mouth. My tongue is still thanking me.

NOVEMBER 15 AT 8:49 A.M.
LIKED BY BETH ANNE CAMPBELL

Bart Swartout in reply to Missy Kirkland: I will be bringing the amazing Bacon Explosion to the BBB Buffet. I don't even have to do the hard work. I know of a place that will make it up ahead of time, and all I need to do is heat it. You're welcome. ☺

NOVEMBER 15 AT 9:05 A.M.
LIKED BY BETH ANNE CAMPBELL AND CHRIS MILFORD.

India Slate in reply to Bart Swartout: Sorry to put a damper on it, but the Bacon Explosion is not my favorite thing … sorry Bart. I know many love it, including my better half. Just not my thing.

NOVEMBER 15 AT 9:32 A.M.

You shut your mouth, India!

> **Ellen O'Rourke in reply to Beth Anne Campbell:** I will definitely be
> researching bacon recipes to bring to the BBB Buffet. Meanwhile, I
> may need to invest in a survival kit I found on Amazon. It has bacon
> balm, bacon drink tabs (to make your water taste like bacon, I guess?),
> bacon car freshener, and, my favorite ... bandages that look like bacon.
> So when you get a paper cut, it looks like you have a little slice of pork
> wrapped around your finger.
>
> NOVEMBER 15 AT 9:44 A.M.
> LIKED BY BETH ANNE CAMPBELL, CAROL BURNS, AND AMELIA WARREN

Between the Yammer announcement and the company-wide email, the
bacon buzz started to swell. This was not going to be your ordinary buffet,
oh no. This would be a historical trough, one that would live on in legend
throughout the years. My head was already spinning with ideas to take this
to the next level. We would have a contest with categories. Questions and
Answers. Flyers everywhere. Christy Dumas even made us a logo.

The buzz was not only happening on Yammer or in my head or in a pan of
bacon frying somewhere in another dimension. It was everywhere.

A few days before the BBBB, I was in the elevator on my way to my fourth-
floor work home with several higher-ups, including a vice president. The
elevator was full, so she didn't pay me any attention, but I paid her a lot of
attention when I heard her asking someone if they heard about this "bacon
thing" on Yammer. I nearly peed myself with delight. Oh yes, madam. I
have indeed heard of this "bacon thing" on Yammer.

The very same day, one of my team members told me he heard people
talking about the BBBB at someone's retirement party. I can't think of anything more appropriate in celebrating one's freedom from decades of labor
than the topic of crunchy fried pork. Can you? The bacon message would
eventually travel out of our work world and into a greater reality, but, for
now, I was tickled pink that people above me on the food chain were no-

ticing. I mean, how could you not? I plastered the Comic Sans posters all over the building. I felt the power in the people.

BRING BACK BACON BUFFET FIRST ANNUAL BACON-OFF AWARDS	
BEST BACON MAIN OR SIDE DISH	
BEST BACON DESSERT	
BEST BACONLESS OR MEATLESS DISH	
MOST ORIGINAL USE OF BACON	
BEST BACON PRESENTATION	
THE HDL LIPITOR AWARD FOR MOST LIKELY TO CAUSE HIGH CHOLESTEROL	

But at the same time, it had to be fun. Along with the potluck itself, I printed ballots (from my home printer, of course) to leave in the breakroom for the tired, hungry masses to vote for their favorite dishes in several categories:

I'll share the results later ... no peeking!

To encourage healthy debate about bacon and the buffet, I also held an email/social media Q&A. As you can imagine, with anything as fantabulous as bacon, there is always controversy. Naysayers are everywhere. I thought this was a good time to enlighten some folks about our most revered of meats.

Q: Dear BBBB Coordinator: The BBBB is great, but I want real change in the cafeteria. I want my bacon bits back! Signed, Occupy Corporate Café

A: Dear OCC: I believe the café has a complaint box; feel free to utilize it. Feel free to not spend your dollars at a place that does not provide the product you want (you should apply this philosophy everywhere, which is why I don't eat at Arby's). The BBBB is friendly in spirit and inclusive and is a gentle way to send a message that we want our bacon bits back without causing a riot.

Q: Dear Bacon Person: Why is bacon so good? It's highly addictive and sometimes I think it should be on the banned narcotics list. Thanks for your reply, @porkiscrack

A: Dear @porkiscrack: I agree 100 percent. The good news for those of us who find our bacon cravings out of control is that bacon isn't available at the supermarket checkout lane. If it were, I would be in bacon rehab right now. You will also notice most grocery store bacon is provided in raw format. This is to prevent addicts such as ourselves from tearing open packages of bacon in the middle of the supermarket and going at them like zombies on brains. We know raw bacon is bad, so we restrain ourselves.

Q: Dear Empress of Bacon: Is raw bacon really bad for us? Signed @ wheretheFismybacon

A: Dear @wheretheFismybacon: I don't think so. I suspect it's just something they tell us as kids so we won't rip open packages of bacon in the middle of the supermarket and go at them like zombies on brains. But I'm not going to test that theory. God sent us frying pans and ovens, so why not use them?

Q: Dear Baconeer: Are there any negatives to bacon? I can't think of any, but I thought, maybe with your vast expertise, you could provide some balance to the Bacon Debate. Sincerely, baconeater.

A: Dear baconeater: There are a few downsides to bacon.

1. *You have to cook it.*

2. *Then your house smells like bacon for a week, which is not inherently a bad thing ... unless you have pets. Then they will hover around you annoyingly until you share.*

3. *You have to share bacon with your pets. Well, you don't HAVE to, but they will not leave you alone until you do. You know how annoying cats are when you are trying to do some work? They sit on your book, your papers, your computer keyboard. Cook up some bacon, and you'll WISH all your cat did was play with the mouse pointer on your laptop screen. Got a Labrador or Golden Retriever? Forget it. You might as well just chuck the entire plate of bacon on the floor. You're not getting any of that shit.*

4. *Bacon runs out. Then you have to go back to the supermarket and buy more.*

5. *But, really, no, there are no negatives to bacon.*

Q: Dear Baconeer: What if I don't eat bacon for religious, moral, or health reasons? Can I still attend the Bring Back Bacon Buffet? Sincerely, Vegetarianeer

A: Dear Vegetarianeer: As long as your religious, moral, or health reasons don't prevent you from being in the vicinity of bacon, you are absolutely encouraged to attend. Personally, I am bringing vegetarian Sesame Noodles with a bacon chaser. Omit the Bacon Chaser, and you are golden.

Q: Dear Bacon Goddess: Why are you allowing non-bacon dishes at the Bring Back Bacon Buffet? Doesn't that defeat the purpose? Signed "Pork Luvver"

A: Dear Pork Luvver: There is no conflict in including non-bacon dishes. There are many bacon-less and meatless foods that may not contain actual pork but still retain the spirit of BBBB. For example, any number of tasty Indian dishes (hint, hint), and of course, my sesame noodles. Who are we to deny potatoes, cheese, pasta, cheese, and cheese?

You may be asking yourself, as Vegetarianeer and Pork Luvver did, why DID I promote meatless dishes at a bacon buffet? This was a calculated decision on my part based on several key factors:

1. We had a lot of people in the company (including many of our outsourcing partners) who either did not eat meat at all or did not eat

pork. Their reasons were varied and included religion, culture, and perceived health. I don't like excluding people from experiencing the spirit of bacon, even if they don't eat it. So, out of respect for the bacon non-eaters, I wanted to make sure they felt welcome, too.

2. There are some tasty non-bacon dishes out there. Why WOULDN'T we indulge? I will have you know, my sesame noodles are FAN-TASTIC, and totally vegetarian (recipe included in the "Recipes" chapter). The only thing that makes my sesame noodles better is crumbled bacon. I could have stirred them into the noodles, but it's easier for me to just keep them separate and let people choose (I'm also a very strong advocate for choice). Win-win. Those who didn't eat meat could indulge, and the bacon lovers could take it to the next level.

3. Bacon is something you can touch, smell, hear, see, and taste, in all its crackly smoked goodness. But it is also a feeling. It's the memory of your mom or dad cooking breakfast. It's your favorite café, where the coffee is freshly brewed and you have breakfast with your friend every Saturday morning. It's feeling the Holy Spirit move through you, even though you hate church, because after the service is a Pancake Brunch (with mountains of bacon on every table). It's the epiphany that you actually LIKE tomatoes and lettuce (which are vegetables), when married with a healthy portion of crispy bacon and a thick slab of mayo. It's those memories you get when you are walking down the street on a cool spring morning and smell one of the neighbors cooking up a pound of fatty pork heaven.

So, yes. I strongly encouraged meatless dishes at a bacon buffet. Sue me.

Beth Anne Campbell has created the ANNUAL BRING BACK BACON BUFFET group: share bacon recipes, stories, injustices, or anything re-motely related to bacon.

Bacon: Any Time, Any Where, Any Dish

NOVEMBER 15 AT 10:22 A.M.
LIKED BY CAROL BURNS, HANNAH MCLEVIN, AND DANA FEY

Tonia Jackson in reply to Beth Anne Campbell: Everywhere I go, I hear people talking about the bacon dishes they are going to bring. It all sounds amazing!

NOVEMBER 15 AT 10:39 A.M.
LIKED BY BETH ANNE CAMPBELL AND SHERYL CLARROLL

Sheila Terada in reply to Beth Anne Campbell: I am in! Tell me when!

NOVEMBER 15 AT 11:30 A.M. FROM IPAD

And so the seed was planted. The corporate health mandate that resulted in bacon bits being removed from the cafeteria salad bar was now an official movement. The peasants were armed with their slow cookers, baking sheets, and plastic bowls, ready to take on the executive overlords.

Those who are about to cook … WE SALUTE YOU!

Chapter 10

Needs More Work

In infinite ways is your flavor a treat;

In the months following BBBB and the managed sourcing initiative, I had many occasions to ponder what went wrong with the corporate changes, and why the removal of bacon from the salad bar (and the overall "health" changes) was so impactful. Of course, the fact that bacon was involved escalated the movement exponentially, but we also saw people getting angry about cheese, mayo, soda pop, and workout equipment. And, as I mentioned earlier, this was not our first health mandate rodeo. This was a fairly regular occurrence, and the decision-makers always succumbed to the laws of supply and demand ... the demand for the "healthy" food plummeted, and, eventually, the supply of desirable food returned. History strongly suggested that *this, too, shall pass*. So why did people get so passionate this time?

The "Bacon movement" was a microcosm of the greater changes going on in the company. The angry protests on the Yammer thread were really a small-scale version of what was happening in the department and company. Changes were being thrust at us without our input. They were not understood, and we were not given sound reasons for why they were being made. Communication was inadequate. People wanted desperately to speak out, but they were either afraid or ignored.

Bacon provided an outlet for people to express frustration about *something*. They were scared to convey their fears and concerns about the outsourcing and other big changes, at least openly. But most of us felt very comfortable venting through social media about bacon and salads and sandwiches. It was safe. Who could possibly be offended by it? Bacon was half a joke, but also, secretly, half the most serious thing at work at the moment. People were afraid to be honest about the changes happening around them … changes that were enormous and very visible and driven fervently by the people in power. But the masses *could* get angry—openly angry—about the changes in the cafeteria. Without any trepidation. Bacon was a way to release their apprehension under the guise of "some silly little thing." But in truth, it wasn't "some silly little thing" and the protest was more about the overall organization than about pork.

Bacon also pulled people together with a common mission. In my now 20 years of corporate life dealing with changes, reorganizations, projects of all sizes, and staff overhauls, I can say with great confidence that, whatever the change may be, it will be much easier if the people involved are in it together. When you don't have a strong leader on a project—someone relatable who is driving the movement with passion, trust, and a stake in its outcome—the project will (at the very least) face unnecessary challenges. At worst, it is destined to fail. When your team members are aligned and informed and have the full support and trust of their leadership, change management is infinitely easier than when they are disjointed, in disagreement, and not doing their job well. This is why bacon worked and the outsourcing and reorganization struggled badly.

The "Baconeers" were aligned. Even the ones who didn't eat salad or even bacon had a common bond: another change that was thrust upon them. Bacon was just the door. It was a portal that opened up to a hot skillet of dissatisfaction that everyone could relate to.

Years later, as I was leaving the company for another opportunity, I relayed the story of Bacon to the new CIO at my going-away party. I talked about Bacon being a microcosm of what was really going on around us with the outsourcing regime and subsequent hell. What resonated with me as I spoke were the many heads nodding around me. My coworkers remembered how shitty they felt, the pits in their stomachs from off-the-charts stress, and the pure relief they got from laughing about bacon or being able to openly get angry about it without fear. Bacon had allowed them to feel like somehow, in some small way, their voices were finally heard. That's really what the BBBB was all about: many confused and disenfranchised people who were under great stress coming together for a common mission.

Bacon, for all intents and purposes, was management's failure.

There were many areas where our executive leadership and upper management got a "needs more work" grade. The most obvious were **trust, change management, employee engagement, and communication.**

Trust

Before you can even fathom addressing any major change, you have to have trust. That takes time. "*Seek first to understand*" someone wise once said (my husband, actually). First, there was the hiring of an outsider into the company in a top position (CIO). Then, the outsider hired a lot of other outsiders, many of them from her own industry—an industry wholly different from our company's. Now, this is not an uncommon thing to do. Sometimes you do need a fresh perspective. But, when you bring in new blood, you have to take time to build trust. Newsflash: *people don't trust you just because you have a title.* They don't trust you because you call yourself a leader or make a lot of money or because they fall somewhere below you on the org chart. You may have done things to earn your title. You may have had great success and you may succeed at this effort too. But right here, right now, you have done *jack shit* to earn the trust and loyalty of your new team. They are total strangers, and they do not trust you yet. It is arrogant to think otherwise.

I realize there is a lot I don't know, as I am not privy to the inner circle of the executive elite. I don't deny decisions can be very tough, and there is a lot of information I lack about what was going on with us at the time from their perspective. But I do know about trust. And, if I am ever allowed in the upper echelons of the business world, I would have a few things to offer on building trust:

DO listen to your people.

Your employees are not idiots. They do have valid concerns about whatever it is you are doing. Pay attention; you might learn something. Ask them questions. They can help you figure it out.

DO acknowledge and understand your employees' feelings and state of mind.

Empathy goes a long way towards trust-building. Yes, a small percentage of people will just be angry and frustrated no matter what. But here's the catch: if they feel like you don't respect their feelings ... if they think you don't care about what they are going through ... that anger and frustration will fester and burn like a dirty sore, and it will infect others who might have been more open to the change and even become your allies. Many of those other people—the ones who might have helped—will give up. You will lose good people. Your lack of emotional respect will be as tangible as a baseball hurled at their stomachs by a Major League pitcher, and they will leave the ballpark.

Also, don't get offended or take it personally when people get upset, angry, or confused. As one of the leads on the EGCI project, I did see and hear re-actions from some of the new executive management team. I heard things like "I don't understand why they are so upset; we are doing this for their own good." Or worse, some got the Dixie Chicks' "Shut Up and Sing" message. I am only one person in a sea of people who were involved at the time, but my take on it was they didn't really want to hear about any con-cerns or issues. They just kept repeating, "We are doing this to help you, so you can focus on projects and not on the day-to-day." I guess they thought this was adequate. Sounds fine, right? *We are doing this to help you.* But the emotional respect was just not there.

So, my advice to anyone in this position is to be empathetic. It doesn't mean you have to stray from your vision (though you might consider input, see previous "DO" about listening to your people). But understand what your people are going through. Acknowledge and accept that they will weather many emotions when dealing with significant change. It's not their fault; just chill and figure out how to make it better.

DO NOT act as if you know everything.

The worst thing a new executive or manager can do coming into a strange crowd is spread their feathers and strut around like they are *The Shit*. I have seen this time and time again. I have heard the same from my network of professionals, friends, and family. This ego show is everywhere, and it is universally hated. Someone comes into a higher position, usually from outside of the company but not always. They start making wholesale changes before first seeking to understand. They don't relate to you. They make minimal—or zero—effort to know you. And, when you question things, innocently and justifiably, you get the clear message THEY know what they are doing.

By the way, this is not just a CIO thing or an upper management thing. There is a small number of people in this world who think their shit doesn't stink. They treat others like dumbass rubes who don't know anything. You know the type: arrogant as hell with egos the size of planets who use patronizing, condescending tones when they communicate. They are too good to listen. They know everything. Sometimes this was the message sent by our leadership. "Shut up and let us make the hard decisions." We know best. I don't know if it was intentional, but it definitely came across as patronizing at times.

DO NOT immediately start making major changes.

Like organization overhauls. Or outsourcing. Take some time to build the trust first. Nothing says "I really don't care about you and I'm going to fuck up your life" like an immediate major reorganization. For fuck's sake, unless the company is going into literal death in the next month, just give it some time.

DO be transparent. And sincere. And honest.

It's OK to say, "We've had some tough years, and this is a way to save some money" or "This is going to be rough, and there will be an adjustment period; I'm not going to kid you." It's OK to say, "I don't know." Not knowing and admitting it is far preferable to withholding information that people might later find out about.

Change Management

I am not a change management expert, but I have been intimately involved with change management from the receiving end for two decades. We are like best friends with benefits. But you don't really need to be an expert to know intuitively what needs to be understood by those most heavily affected. *What the hell are we doing? Why the hell are we doing this? How the hell are we going to do this? And what the hell is my life going to look like when this is all done?*

What the hell are we doing?

This is the first question that arises in a change management situation. What is happening? In our case, the answer was *outsourcing*, but they didn't call it that. *Outsourcing* was a dirty word at the time. So, they tried to temper it by calling it *managed sourcing*. BZZZZZ! *I'm sorry; you are incorrect. Thank you for playing.* The fact that anyone had to change the commonly accepted term was in itself a red flag. Were they trying to hide something? Again, we are not dumb, brainless rubes. See "Trust" above.

But OK. Semantics. The real problem was that for many people, the "What the hell are we doing?" didn't make any sense. The explanation we heard over and over was we were going to farm out the day-to-day support of our software and technology to an outsourcing company so we, the company folk, would have more time for project work. On my team, this wasn't totally out of the realm of believability. Oh, I had MANY reservations about other things (see *How the hell are we going to do this?* below). But my team was already involved in several large high-profile projects. We had been in project mode for the last five years or more. And we had other very large projects coming down the road in the near future. So, generally, a few of us understood the *What* to a certain degree.

But there were more than 500 people in the department. And many of them, maybe the majority, did not do heavy project work. Their jobs WERE the day-to-day support being outsourced. So, the *What* did not resonate at all. They knew they didn't have projects in their area, so the alternative was they would be *repurposed*. Transferred somewhere else where more bodies were needed, on some big project on another IT team that was short-staffed. Except people and skills aren't immediately transferable. It's not plug and play. Some of the skill sets needed on these other projects were rather comprehensive. It wasn't that most of the employees who were being shuffled *couldn't* learn—they absolutely could, over time, with training and experience. The "experience" part usually being the day-to-day support, which we were not going to be doing any more. See the problem?

So, the *What* ... it didn't make much sense to anyone.

Why the hell are we doing this?

The *Why* was equally unclear. What we heard over and over was that the poor, the tired, the overworked peasants would be free, free, FREEEE from the dull, repetitive maintenance routine. We could finally be unshackled from those pedestrian support tasks and let loose on new adventures, namely large multi-year projects fraught with budget constraints, scheduling nightmares, long days and weekend work, and frequent burnout. Oh yes, please sign me up!

But, as we have pointed out, not everyone even had projects lined up. And, mostly, the work wasn't really dull or repetitive, and people enjoyed doing it. So, the *Why* was ludicrous, too. *Hi, I've been doing my job for 30 years, and doing it well; I have great relationships with the business team I serve, I respond quickly and efficiently, and, oh, by the way I'm going to be retiring in five years so it doesn't really make sense for me to make wholesale career changes right now. So, tell me again how this makes sense?* But the answers they got from the outsourcing pushers were inadequate, and the uncertainty spread like warm mayonnaise on a BLT.

How the hell are we going to do this?

100 percent, this was my biggest concern. I wasn't afraid of losing my job. Aside from the reality that the assignment leading my team's transition was a blazing inferno of chaos, my real reservations were about the timeline and the resources taking over.

It's like those TV shows where they build a house in a week for some deserving family. This is what we were trying to do. We were trying to build an entire city in three months, except we didn't have an unlimited budget or every local expert in their field at our disposal, or renowned specialists ready at a moment's notice to help us with the challenges. Oh, and, by the way, this wasn't our only job during the transition period. We still had to keep everything running. We still had to work the current projects we were on, support the systems, manage teams, respond to crises, and many other activities consumed our daily (and sometimes nightly) worlds. Just trying to get the right people from our team as well as from the transition team in the same conference room for a few days, let alone weeks, was nearly impossible.

We couldn't even tackle the impossibility of scheduling until we had lead resources from the outsourcing team. Which we've already seen was an endless in and out of so-called experts who apparently have a lot of sick relatives.

In spite of our constant pleas to the upper management and executive staff to help with the unreasonableness of the schedule, it was not adjusted to accommodate reality. In spite of us begging to pull back some of our bigger systems and keep the support in house, most of them went through the "transition." And suffered for it.

What is my life going to look like when all of this is done?

You won't lose your job.

> *(but you may be placed in areas in which you have zero experience)*

> *(the résumé update workshop is just a coincidence)*

You won't get laid off.

> *(but we are going to offer many "incentives" for you to leave. Cutting costs and company headcount has been the goal all along; what the hell did you think?)*

> *(Early Retirement Incentive Announcement!)*

The outsourcing team will be just as dedicated as you are, and the turnover will slow way down.

> *(wait … ANOTHER person quit?)*

You won't have to do any day-to-day support work.

> *(shaking your head as yet another day-to-day support ticket comes into your email)*

The outsourcing team will run things just as well as you did.

> *(not in all areas, but in some … although it will take a few years to get there)*

You'll get to spend more time on exciting projects!

> *(outsourcing won't actually help with the many challenges you are experiencing in your projects … SORRY NOT SORRY!)*

To my knowledge, no one did get laid off in the strictest sense as a direct result of the outsourcing. But many, many people were driven out. There were lots of early retirements. Lots of "found a better opportunity" situations. Many people saw the door open and started to look through the crack for something else, even though they might not have walked out until later. A lot of people tolerated the almost intolerable stress because they couldn't leave or were afraid to leave because they still had families to feed and bills to pay. A lot of manager-types fell into this bucket. A couple of them who were closer to the executive chain of command than I was confided in me that they had clearly received the "support us or else" message. They felt they had no other choice.

Eventually, the workload and new processes settled in, but it took a long, long time. Things were never the same, and not always in a good way. People didn't get laid off per se, but they did lose their jobs and, in some cases, their spirit. Retraining people for other jobs was difficult and pushed a lot of people out (and I wonder if this wasn't the goal—even the expectation—all along). The outsourcing team had pockets of dedicated individuals, and they were all good people just doing their jobs. But turnover offshore was high, and we paid the price when the few experienced people in a support area would move onto other opportunities outside of our company (which happened far too often). We continued to do a lot (in some cases, all) of the real support work while the outsourcing team became very adept at the routine tasks. Many of them could have been as good as the company team if they had stuck around long enough. But that's generally not how offshore technical support works, in my opinion.

The company employees did get to work more on projects, and they were exciting, if by "exciting" you mean long, over-budget, crunched into unreasonable timelines, resources working to burnout, and with frustrated business partners. And we still didn't have enough people to staff them.

Employee Engagement

What is employee engagement? Spoiler: it can be different for everyone. This is why it is important to ask and to listen. It is critical to understand so you can respond accordingly. And it might change over time. It's a bit of a dance sometimes, but you've taken a big step by just asking your team what they need and why they are not engaged. The simple acts of valuing their thoughts and listening actually go a long way toward more engaged employees.

I can't tell you how to fix low employee engagement scores on a survey or how to boost morale for each person. Like I said, it's different for everyone, and your work culture may need something entirely different than mine did. It's probably easier to tell you what doesn't work, generally. For example, the next time your team or department or company is experiencing low employee engagement, don't let someone attempt to fix this by scheduling a picnic or an after-work bar event or baseball game or escape room. These are great team activities, and I have enjoyed them all. They can be wonderful bonding experiences for a stable, engaged team, but they are usually mutually exclusive from employee engagement. Now, if it's an intimate picnic or dinner where you are actually talking to people and listening to their feedback to better understand how to help, then sure. Absolutely. But I have been to a lot of big picnics and dinners in my time, and rarely have they been about listening and understanding. They are mostly about having fun or the often-misguided notion that employees aren't fulfilled because they don't have company-sponsored golf, grilled hot dogs, or beer.

When Maya came into power, she opened the door for access to social media previously banned. We were star struck. We could look at Facebook or Twitter over lunch without getting the dreaded "THIS WEBSITE IS PROHIBITED" message that made us feel like we just accessed a child pornography site. And I won't lie: it was great! BBBB would never have happened but for access to Yammer. But it wasn't a solution to low employee engagement.

We had a couple of picnics, which were fun and appreciated. But they didn't provide any solutions on employee engagement. They didn't address our feelings of not being valued, or the long hours, high stress, fear about losing jobs, concerns about the outsourcing transition, processes that were impossible to follow, or lack of feeling of personal or team accomplishment, etc. At best, they were stress relievers, but I can tell you a few people even found the picnics stressful, wondering if there was an ulterior motive. *What's the agenda? How is this helping?*

To their credit, Maya and some of the directors did (for a while) attempt to hold some more "intimate" lunches with department team members. I attended a couple of them, and honest feedback from people was sparse. I know some of them had very strong thoughts because I had talked about it with them outside of these gatherings. But there still wasn't the trust needed for most people to feel comfortable being open with virtual strangers in high positions. Those of us who did speak out had learned our voices were not heard, our input not really accepted, our unease swept under the rug. It felt like our words were just dismissed as complaining, as if the people in charge were just going through the motions without any real desire to hear, process, or react to the concerns of the masses. *Shut up and sing.* So we just sang, and most people stopped trying to send a message to the outsourcing leadership.

I don't want to come down too hard on Maya and the other executives and directors on this. Not understanding what employee engagement is all about is not something exclusive to them. It is rampant. I talk to people *all the time* whose leaders never take the time to really understand their employees and why they are or aren't happy. Some just don't know how. A lot of them still use 1950s authoritarian management styles where they think their employees should just consider themselves lucky to have jobs at all, let alone one that pays well and they get to sit in a nice office all day. Others are borderline (or not even borderline) dictators who rule by fear and whose only goal is to do whatever they need to do to make a profit, as long as it's not illegal. Making profit is a great goal. Yes, yes, yes, yes, we all know companies have to make money. We are not stupid. But what they all don't realize is, whatever the goal, it will get reached much faster when you have employees who *want* to do good work for you. Not because they have to. Not because you threaten them or push stupid logic about profit and revenue on them. Not because you make them feel guilty about wanting something better. Not because you remind them of how much they are getting paid. Not because you have a title, a degree, or yell the loudest.

They do it because they are fulfilled and happy and feel they are a *part of that success*, not just a means to it.

That one is worth repeating: they do it because *they feel they are a part of that success, not just a means to it.* They are invested in the company because they feel the company is invested in them. They are engaged.

Communication

The first mistake was letting the CIO and her new hires deliver the messages. Remember, trust was nonexistent. The atmosphere was a cloud of the exact opposite of trust. And, if I am being honest, the ability to connect with the audience was severely lacking. Our leadership was giving us some information; I cannot deny that. But there was zero connection. They didn't speak our "language," and they had about as much charisma between all of them as a dried turnip. It was like going on a blind date and wanting to leave the restaurant by the time the first drinks arrived. The chemistry was nil.

On a regular and frequent basis, the entire department would gather in the auditorium while Maya and her staff showed us slide after slide, trying to convince us how great outsourcing would be. And many of us just sat there clenching our teeth, wanting to scream out every time they said something that just didn't make sense. Why should we believe them? They had zero emotional connection. We just did not relate. I remember suggesting to my boss they let our director, Maggie Shupert, take over the Town Hall. Maggie had history with us, and she was a damn good communicator. When she spoke, it was always with sincerity. She had an inherent sense of empathy in her voice, and I always felt like I was talking with my favorite big sister (if I had a big sister). When you talked with Maggie, you felt like she really listened, and she really understood and respected your position. Once or twice she did briefly address the team at our gatherings, but those moments were few and far between. Not enough to overcome a trust gap the size of the Palo Duro Canyon.

So the information continued to flow, albeit badly and with holes. The messages were not adequately delivered or addressed. And throughout all of the trust, change management, and employee engagement challenges, communication suffered through it all. The *Who, What, When,* and *How* of the messages were mostly a shit show of how NOT to spread the word. Again, this gap is not exclusive to this executive management team or company. But inadequate communication was a big part of why this effort did not go well and why resistance was so high.

And, oddly enough, communication was one of the main reasons the BBBB movement was so successful. It's amazing what can happen when you let people speak without judgment and then react accordingly. Somehow, Bacon succeeded in bringing hundreds of people together in harmony and in general agreement where highly paid executives and directors and managers could not.

That, my friends, is what I mean by "the spirit of bacon."

Chapter 11

The Bring-back-bacon Buffet

Oh bacon, I love thee, and can't wait to eat!

Beth Anne Campbell in ANNUAL BRING BACK BACON BUFFET:
The BRING BACK BACON BUFFET is in FULL SWING in the fourth-floor Business Center at corporate headquarters! Response has been phenomenal! Stop by and try some delicious bacon-full and bacon-less dishes! DON'T FORGET TO VOTE! Ballots are available in the business center, or you can send your ballot to me via email.

NOVEMBER 18 AT 8:38 A.M.

If this is an audiobook, you may hear angels singing right now.

At this point in the tale I'm supposed to say, "I wasn't really sure what to expect." Then there would be some humbling words elaborating on my uncertainty about how this would play out, followed by a build up to the surprise climax. But that would be a lie. There was no surprise. I knew this was going to be good. I had talked with dozens and dozens of people about bacon and health mandates and forced change and their low "employee engagement." I had overheard people talking about bacon in the elevator and in conference rooms. I had listened to the cries of the unfulfilled masses. I had been given bacon gifts and sent scores of bacon-themed memes, food photos, and jokes. BBBB had been added to our company Wiki. The internal social media had exploded like the fatty tip of a thick-sliced slab of hickory-smoked pork belly.

No doubt in my mind. No doubt at all.

> **Kevin Weeper in reply to Beth Anne Campbell:** I imagine it smells phenomenal on the fourth floor right now. If only I didn't have meetings at the Portland facility today. Maybe they wouldn't even miss me …
>
> NOVEMBER 18 9:38 A.M.
> LIKED BY BETH ANNE CAMPBELL AND CHRISTY DUMAS

> **India Slate in reply to Beth Anne Campbell:** YESSS!! Our peaceful bacon revolt has claimed a victory! Power to the people; power to the pork!
>
> NOVEMBER 18 AT 9:49 P.M.
> LIKED BY JUAN GRABARRA, CAROL BURNS, AND CHRIS MILFORD

> **Beth Anne Campbell in reply to Kevin Weeper:** I don't even notice it now, but this morning it was all bacony goodness as soon as I got off the elevator!
>
> NOVEMBER 18 AT 10:09 P.M.
> LIKED BY CAROL BURNS

Indeed.

As I hoisted my sesame noodle-filled slow cooker off the elevator and onto the fourth floor at 7:30 a.m., the air was already filled with the fragrance of pan-fried pork. An invisible, savory fog caressed my nostrils and hypnotized me into a state where I could only recognize positive things. I could actually taste bacon in the back of my throat, on that little soft palate between the mouth and nose. This is normally where I sense the first sign of a cold virus, but, today, it was nothing but pure joy.

The business center was already being filled with a sea of bacon delights. If Willy Wonka's factory had been about bacon rather than candy, this would have been the Great Bacon Room. Augustus Gloop would have jumped into the warm river of bacon grease and had no trouble whatsoever sliding up the pipe. Veruca Salt would have been perfectly fine because there is no garbage chute for bacon (what a horrible thought). Violet Beauregarde would have bloated up but only temporarily—water retention from a lot of salt after chewing her bacon dinner gum (complete with maple bacon donut for dessert). And Mike Teevee would have been ELATED to shrink so small that a single slice of bacon could last him all week!

Charlie? Charlie would have inherited the factory to end all factories. Grandpa Joe and Grandma Josephine—and Grandpa George and Grandma Georgina—would all live out their days under the warm umbrella of salty cured pork. This is how I want to die. Surrounded by pork bellies and bacon bits and Oompa Loompas.

> **Bart Swartout ANNUAL BRING BACK BACON BUFFET:** The Bacon Explosion is upon its altar for all to hail! ☺ Anyone who wants to try it, it's awaiting your taste buds in the fourth-floor business center!
>
> NOVEMBER 18 AT 11:05 A.M.

> **Bart Swartout in reply to Darrin Potter:** Also, there is a boatload of amazing stuff here, mostly bacon-themed.
>
> NOVEMBER 18 AT 11:06 A.M.

Bart's Bacon Explosion was the heart of the buffet. It was layer upon layer of pure pork madness nestled in a cozy blanket of woven bacon. I wished I could weave a bacon blanket so big it would cover my bed and I could snuggle up under the smoky comfort and have little piggy dreams. But there is no way in hell anyone could weave a bacon blanket as big as a bed, because seriously, how long could you actually work on it before you got hungry and just started noshing on the thing? Three minutes, tops.

Kasha Finn in reply to Bart Swartout: Please send a slab of the glorious Bacon Explosion over to us peons who don't work at corporate HQ. We are drooling all over our keyboards reading the BBBB thread.

NOVEMBER 18 AT 11:16 A.M.

LIKED BY MICKEY RIVES

Beth Anne Campbell in reply to Kasha Finn: Karen, we feel for you ... however, there is nothing stopping you from organizing your own local BRING BACK BACON BUFFET! The response has been overwhelming. Bacon is one of the BEST ways to bring about employee engagement!

NOVEMBER 18 AT 11:23 A.M.

LIKED BY TONIA JACKSON, KASHA FINN, AND MICKEY RIVES

Kasha Finn in reply to Beth Anne Campbell: That might just be in the plan!

NOVEMBER 18 AT 11:29 A.M.

One of my few regrets with this whole event was that I wasn't able to help coordinate our satellite locations. I am but one woman. But, even though we were limited to a single building, we had tons of support from across the state. They had not organized their own BBBB, but they were rooting for us and were there in spirit.

By 8 a.m., the "Bacon Center" was filled with a spread to end all spreads. Charlene's amazing bacon cheese ball stood like a trophy on the counter nearest the south entrance of the room. It greeted the awestruck visitors like a beacon of hope. It was far better than I had imagined when she sent me the recipe a few days earlier, the one I had spoken about on Yammer. And she did not flank this fortress of cow and pig with cheap cardboard-like crackers, oh no. She went all out with RITZ because can you really put anything less with your layers of cream cheese, more cheese, and REAL bacon bits??? Charlene is a master Baconeer, and she knew how to honor her pork masterpiece.

Juan Grabarra brought a work of art known only as "Bacon Bake." This memorable dish included OVER TWO DOZEN EGGS. There are not many foods that even come close to bacon in my cold heart. Homemade buttercream frosting. Fresh sourdough bread slathered with real butter. Mom's meatball recipe. And Eggs. A sea of spheres-o'-delight were cracked and whisked with mounds of cheddar cheese and an infinity of bacon. The secret ingredient (as if one could even dare to ask for it to be any better) was hash browns: shredded potatoes that are crispy and greasy on the outside, but soft and tender within. The perfect complement to crispy bacon bits and soft scrambled eggs.

Naomi Bronkowski brought chocolate-covered bacon. WHAT IS THIS SORCERY? I had never even imagined such a thing! I am almost ashamed to admit that in all of my vast dreams of chocolate and of bacon, the two were never coupled. But, oh, what a marriage this was! Creamy dark chocolate caressed the fleshy thighs of strip after strip of bacon. I know the salty/sweet combination is not for everyone. I have listened to my better half fake dry-heave every time I mention putting Raisinets or M&M's into my popcorn at the movie theater. But there is a market, and I am a fan, so this delightful combo resonated with me. I wished I could have officiated this wedding, but I happily enjoyed the reception.

Perhaps my favorite bacon dessert was some sort of chocolate chip cookie with bacon in it. My Spidey senses also detected cornflake cereal. I am a total sucker for a well-made chocolate-chip cookie. Must use fresh ingredients. If you are one of those people who uses fake butter, or who cuts down on the sugar to make the cookie (*gag*) healthier—I'm talking to you, Mom—then just shut this book down right now. Go to the grocery store; get yourself some free-range eggs, organic butter, and enough brown sugar and cane sugar to fill a wheelbarrow. Pick up some real vanilla, not that imitation shit. Then come back and resume reading with your dignity intact.

I don't know who made these discs of delight. There were definitely corn flakes in there. I have used corn flakes in place of crisped rice cereal for decades in my marshmallow delights, so I am extremely sensitive to the superior flavor of corn flaked cereal mixed with sugar. And the bacon just took them over the edge. A fine chocolate-chip cookie is a wondrous thing. Sprinkle in some crushed corn flakes and it becomes something to be revered. Add some crumbled bacon bits and now you have the rainbow unicorn of cookies. I wanted to sacrifice myself to those salty sweet angels but, instead, I just ate two or seven of them.

> **Beth Anne Campbell in ANNUAL BRING BACK BACON BUFFET:** I especially appreciate bacony goodness that is hand-delivered to my desk. Thanks @CGurley and @DGurley for dropping off maple bacon cupcakes with maple frosting. They are GORGEOUS! They even have sugar crystals adorning the bacon tuft atop the swirled icing!

I lied. The corn flake cereal chocolate-chip bacon rainbow unicorn cookies were not my favorite bacon dessert. They were ONE of my favorite bacon desserts, tied with one of my other favorite bacon desserts: maple-bacon cupcakes with maple frosting. These works of art were donated by Camille and Drake Gurley, who were not even at work. The cause was so important that Camille came in from her vacation to deliver their contribution. They were so beautiful. The maple frosting was a tuft of love on top of a little mound of maple-bacon comfort cake. Coarse sugar crystals were sprinkled on top of the icing like diamonds. A chunk of bacon was delicately slid into the frosting in a presentation almost too good to eat. *Almost.* I must admit, I was skeptical at first. Bacon cupcakes? *Would that even work?* Just kidding. I knew this was going to be amazing right from the get-go. Really, what is a maple-bacon cupcake but a hand-held version of an excellent pancakes and bacon breakfast? And they were incredible.

The best part about these cupcakes was that Camille wasn't able to drop them off until late afternoon. The Gurleys' inconvenient schedule was my bliss. I had one of these decadent wonders just before I put the rest of them in the break room. It was already quitting time for many people, so the crowds had died down. Most of the bacon pleasures were long gone. The lights in the breakroom were already dimmed in preparation for the upcoming weekend, when the halls would be silent but still smelling of pork. I was ready to go home myself. I looked at the platter of maple-bacon mini-cakes, and I knew this would not be our last rendezvous.

Speaking my truth: I came into work on Saturday and scarfed down three more of those puppies. Let's just say, maybe I wanted to catch up on some paperwork. OK? I had to be there anyway. Allegedly. The outsourcing project was still in full swing, still Hell, and I was behind due to my commitment to the masses and their piggy protest. It was a long weekend day and of course I got a little hungry. Those muffins were just sitting there. If I had left them for Monday, probably the cleaning staff would have thrown them away. They might have gone stale and then all that bacon would have gone to waste. I couldn't even imagine such a thing. So, I made a sacrifice for the cause.

Every one of them was worth it. And in my defense, they were smallish cupcakes. Don't judge.

Jane Blacksmith brought Cheesy Bacon Potatoes for the trifecta of drool. And bless her heart, she included an option in her recipe to omit the bacon to make the dish vegetarian. Why anyone would want to *omit bacon* is beyond me (I can't even write the words without my hands shaking), but I respect most lifestyle choices. Jane's slow cooker of awesome won the award for Best Bacon Presentation. She brought a cute little pink pig and displayed it in an empty slow cooker. Sorry for the pig, but it was adorable. Jane worked for the title, and it paid off.

Christy Dumas brought Bacon Buckeyes. For those of you non-Midwesterners, a Buckeye in this context is not an Ohio State Alumnus, nor the nutlike seed of the buckeye shrub or tree (although these buckeyes did resemble the nut). 'Round these parts, a "Buckeye" is a ball of sweet peanut butter confection dipped in chocolate. Every year at Christmas, my sister Sue makes buckeyes and brings them to the family gathering. I will beg her to roll them in bacon next time, because I just remembered how amazing Christy's little bacon-PB-chocolate nut-clouds were. Bacon Buckeyes were second place in several of the voting categories, but, in my opinion, they get extra honors for Hometown Nostalgia and Best Use of Bacon and Peanut Butter together.

There were so many other bacon masterpieces; I almost peed my pants in delight as the dishes kept pouring in. Bacon coiled up in colorful appetizer wraps, bacon swimming in soft, golden corn muffins, bacon subs, bacon pasta, several varieties of bacon cookies and salads and cheesy potatoes. Bacon chili, because why the fuck not? Bacon with beans, bacon with tuna, pumpkin bacon, bacon dip, and brownies and sausage. Bacon with cold potatoes, bacon with hot potatoes, even deep-fried bacon (THANK YOU ROB MASCHEVITZ !!!). There were pretzels wrapped in bacon, chocolate-covered bacon, slow cookers galore, casserole after casserole filled with bacon dreams, and of course my vegetarian Sesame Noodles with bacon on the side (they were amazing, if I do say so myself).

And last, but certainly not least … the man who started it all, Darrin Potter, who brought in a big pan of JUST BACON. Darrin, I bow to your originality and also your diligence in identifying the egregious removal of bacon bits from the salad bar and starting this whole glorious mess. "Just Bacon" seems so simple, and yet so appropriate. Because, even among all of these stunning bacon successes, there is nothing like the experience of a pure strip of unadulterated bacon rapture.

The votes were counted, and, at the end of the day, the Bacon Explosion and Naomi's chocolate-covered bacon were fan favorites. My Spicy Sesame Noodles garnered an award, but methinks maybe there was some bias there, and also, there really weren't many baconless dishes. And I wasn't really upset about it. Personally, I voted for the Pumpkin Éclair in the Meatless category.

BRING BACK BACON BRUNCH FIRST ANNUAL BACON-OFF AWARDS	
BEST BACON MAIN OR SIDE DISH	BACON EXPLOSION (Bart Swartout)
BEST BACON DESSERT	CHOCOLATE-COVERED BACON (OINK) (Naomi Bronkowski)
BEST BACONLESS OR MEATLESS DISH	SPICY SESAME NOODLES (Beth Anne Campbell)
MOST ORIGINAL USE OF BACON	CHOCOLATE COVERED BACON (Naomi Bronkowski)
BEST BACON PRESENTATION	CHEESY POTATOES WITH BACON (Jane Blacksmith)
THE HDL LIPITOR AWARD FOR MOST LIKELY TO CAUSE HIGH CHOLESTEROL	BACON EXPLOSION (Bart Swartout)

But the best part of the day wasn't even the food.

What? Are you CRAZY, girlfriend? It's a BACON BUFFET, for Pete's sake, how can the food not be the best part? Who ARE you?

The best part of the day was having all these people come together as a family—eight hours of laughter, good food, good conversation, and the sense we had accomplished something. I heard so much positivity that day, more than I had heard in the past year. People would pass me in the hall and make little comments like "Now THIS is what employee engagement is all about!" or "Best idea ever!" or "We should do this more often!" We laughed a ton (as much as we could with our stuffed bellies; I mean, we were hurtin'). People outside of the IT department contributed and engaged in conversation, and I got to meet people I only knew from Yammer or not even at all. Personally, I was on cloud nine. It ranks as one of the top five days in my life to this day. But, as a work family, it didn't get any better than this. We had a mission, we accomplished the mission, and, no matter what the ultimate outcome for poor bacon on the salad bar, we had sent a message loud and clear.

And it felt really, really good.

Q: *Dear Bringer of All That is Bacon: I think I've reached a point where I don't want to eat anything with bacon on it for a while. I can't even look at the stuff. I'm thinking about giving it up for a bit ... an hour, at least. Is there such a thing as bacon-saturation? (no name given)*

A: *Dear Anonymous: There is no such thing as "bacon saturation." What you are experiencing is commonly known as "The Bacon Bloat." Bacon is very salty, and, under normal conditions, should not be consumed more than five times per day. Due to the Bring Back Bacon Buffet trough, you have probably consumed the equivalent of a month's worth of tasty fried pork plus a gallon or so of liquid to quench the salt-inspired thirst. As you so well predicted, this will go away in an hour or so, leaving you again with a normal craving for bacon. Luckily for you, there are still plenty of tasty bacon cookies left in the fourth-floor business center.*

Chapter 12

The Aftermath

Monday, November 21, work voicemail

Hi, Beth, this is Joe Rand. My wife Alice works in IT at "The Company." She's been telling me about the bacon protest potluck, and I think it's great—funniest thing ever. I don't know if you know Brent Foley; he's a feature writer with the Citizen Tribune. Anyway, he's a friend of mine; we were having a beer over the weekend, and I mentioned the bacon thing, and, well, he just loved it. He'd really like to talk to you. So please call me back and let me know if I can hook him up. Here's my number.

Monday, November 21, email

To: Beth Anne Campbell
From: Tim Fenstermaker, IT
Subject: FW: FW: FW: Bacon Protest Story for the *Citizen Tribune*

Hi, Beth ... just wanted to pass this on, see chain below. This went to Media who sent it to Legal. Just want you to be careful; this is serious. Watch your back.

Tim

Forwarded email:

> **From:** Arthur Fenstermaker
> **To:** Tim Fenstermaker
> **Subject:** FW: FW: Bacon Protest Story for the *Citizen Tribune*
>
> FYI. We're just ignoring this for now, as is the media team. Just wanted you to be aware.
>
> Thanks,
> Art

Forwarded email:

> **From:** Media Group
> **To:** Legal Group
> **Subject:** FW: Bacon Protest Story for the *Citizen Tribune*
>
> Has anyone been contacted by Brent Foley (writer for the *Citizen Tribune*)? We got this odd email from him about a bacon protest. Does anyone know anything about this? Let me know if you do. Not sure what he is talking about. Let's hope he just goes away.
>
> Thanks,
> Joan

Forwarded email:

> **From:** Brent Foley, Citizen Tribune
> **To:** Media Group
> **Subject:** Bacon Protest Story for the *Citizen Tribune*
>
> Hello all,
>
> I heard there was a big bacon protest going on at the company, something about bacon bits removed from the salad bar? A friend of mine whose wife works there mentioned it, and I wanted to follow up. I would

love to do a story on this in the *Tribune*. It's right up my alley. Who can I talk with to get more information?

Feel free to call or email. Thank you!

Brent Foley
Head Feature Writer
Citizens Tribune
(555) 555-5555

Tim Fenstermaker worked in my department. His nephew is Arthur, and Arthur worked in Legal. It pays to have friends like this. Not that I was worried, but I definitely wanted to get on top of it. Also, under what rock had Media and Legal been living that they did not have an inkling as to what was going on? People were talking about the bacon protest at retirement parties. My neighbor across the street knew about it. I guess I should be thankful, because they might very well have shut down this mission before it happened if they had been a little more hip on the company goings on.

As it were, I had to slow down this crazy train ASAP.

Email:

From: Beth Anne Campbell
To: Legal Group, Media Group
Subject: FW: FW: FW: FW: Bacon Protest Story for the Citizen Tribune

Hello,

I can shed some light on this. I work in IT, and what Brent is referring to is the Bring Back Bacon Buffet (potluck) held last Friday. This was a very lighthearted "protest" that grew out of a post on the company social media a couple weeks ago, when bacon bits were removed from the salad bar as part of the corporate "health" mandate. The entire post and comments are on Yammer, free to view if you want more information.

I have not had any contact with Mr. Foley, nor do I intend to. He got my name from a friend whose wife works in the IT department. The friend/husband of my coworker left me a voice message over the weekend. I have not responded nor do I have any intention of doing so.

This was just a friendly, tongue-in-cheek potluck we held in the fourth-floor business center. That's as far as it went or will go.

Please let me know if you need any further information; I am happy to discuss.

Thank you,
Beth Anne Campbell

My experience has always been that, if I am transparent with people and give them information, it will be much better than withholding or making something up. I knew we hadn't done anything wrong, but I also knew these things had a way of escalating unnecessarily when people started coming to their own conclusion. So, I sent the explanation email to Media and Legal. I never did get a response from anyone, there was no follow up, I didn't get in trouble. And the whole thing just died down and went away.

Well, OK, it didn't really die down and go away. It never turned into a media or legal frenzy, but ...

Several days after the Bring Back Bacon Buffet, bacon bits mysteriously returned to the salad bar at the corporate cafeteria. They came at a premium similar to the other company facilities, but at least they were back. $0.50 was a small price to pay for such a big victory.

Speaking of victory, a couple weeks after BBBB, the following post appeared in Yammer, from the senior vice president who had been behind the health mandate in the cafeteria. He was the one who was responsible for the ultimately disappearance of our favorite pork product.

Don M. Steward—Bacon Bits and Cheese

Folks, I wanted to take a moment and address a few things about our cafeteria here at corporate HQ. First, if anyone disagreed with the Health Initiative or its approach, please accept my apology. We always welcome your feedback, and, as a result of your comments, we have made some changes. As always, we are trying to provide an environment in which health is a priority. But, of course, we will certainly make mistakes as we figure it out. I wish I could snap my fingers and make everyone healthy, but, obviously, that isn't realistic. We will continue to work toward a universally supportive approach, so please continue to let us know how we are doing. We do want to learn and adapt as we move forward.

DECEMBER 1 AT 4:17 A.M.

LIKED BY JANET HOLMES, MICKEY RIVES, LANA M. MUNCHAUSEN, AND NINE OTHERS

I give a lot of credit to Mr. Steward. He's a nice guy, and, yes, as you would imagine, very fit. A couple years after the whole outsourcing thing, we got a video message from Don M. Steward letting us know Maya was leaving the company. It was a very odd communication. For one, it was a video announcement of a high-level staff departure, and that had never (to my knowledge) happened before. Second, the entire video was of Don sitting next to Maya as he announced her departure, then her stating she had taken a position elsewhere. I don't really know for sure if this was her choice or if she was pushed or pressured to leave, but my money is on the latter. It was a very uncomfortable video and sort of felt like I was watching a dad publicly reprimanding his daughter for sneaking out after curfew and getting caught. But one thing is for sure: Don M. Steward was my ultimate hero in that very moment.

I gained a lot of respect for Mr. Steward when he issued his apology.

Ron Upton in reply to Don M. Steward: As someone who brown-bags it most days (due to dietary restrictions I must undertake), I was not affected directly by the bacon issue (confession: I did spend a few days in mourning when the coffee shop stopped serving ice cream). Regardless, I am grateful for what Corporate has done regarding health and wellness. I'm especially thankful for the Wellness Center, very underappreciated, and the company continues to make improvements. I think it is a great facility and wish more people would take advantage of it. As we near the end of this year and people start putting together their New Year's Resolutions, consider adding physical activity to the list. The Wellness Center does get busy during lunch, but, the rest of the day, it's pretty dead. I'm often there in the pre-work hours timeframe and it's near empty.

DECEMBER 2 AT 9:07 A.M.

Jan Heyou in reply to Don M. Steward: Don, we appreciate your "weighing in" (ha ha) on the health topic. It must be hard to balance company initiatives and employee responsibility. Most of us are grateful Corporate is willing to try new things and also adjust based on feedback.

DECEMBER 2 AT 10:34 A.M.

Beth Anne Campbell in reply to Don M. Steward: As the most verbal proponent of bacon, I will offer that I think ... no, I KNOW ... the greater company community can come up with some creative ideas to promote health in a way that is fun, motivational, and well-received. I've already seen a few of them on the bacon posts, and I think if we all have the opportunity to contribute ideas, we can make a difference.

How about a Yammer group for Healthy Lifestyle? A place where people can provide suggestions (like, what would they like to see healthy in the cafe), share tips, tell their success (or failure) stories, ask questions of their peers, etc.? Hey, I'm a chunky girl who needs some more health in my life; I'd be posting every lunch hour! :-)

DECEMBER 2 AT 10:56 A.M.

LIKED BY DANA FEY, MICKEY RIVES, JANET HOLMES, AND EIGHT OTHERS

My intent was never to discourage anyone from trying to be healthier. My concern and those of others was more the way Corporate went about it. And (since health directives in the cafeteria were not unfamiliar) the way they went about it *and* their impeccably awful timing. I considered taking the reins myself and starting a Yammer group. Maybe I could do with fitness and overall health (my own included) what I had done with bacon. But, as things go, *After Bacon* I got caught up again in the frenzy of Information Technology chaos and it never happened. It is one of my few regrets.

I continued to get comments about "that bacon thing" for a very long time.

A little over a year *AB*, we held the second Bring Back Bacon Buffet. It was definitely different than the first, in that there wasn't the type of passion-fueled-by-anger that had driven BBBB1. Both were happy occasions (I mean, it's BACON), but the original BBBB was born out of a mission, a sense that we all had something to fight for (or against). The second buffet was born more out of a need to lift our spirits. By this time, we were heavily into the outsourcing effort. Still struggling. Still working on big, long projects. Still dealing with frustrated business partners. Still heavily supporting many of the outsourcing teams. We needed a morale booster. What better way to bring a sparkle back into the downtrodden than to eat tasty food with lots of pork accents?

BBBB2 was in *some* ways even better than the original BBBB. Participation from our outsourcing partners was much greater. We had become friends with the team leads who were onsite at headquarters, and they were dealing with the same frustrations, the same pressure from management, and the same high turnover from the offshore team as we were. Part of our development team had moved across the street to a satellite building, so they held a simultaneous BBBB2, thereby expanding the power of bacon across space as well as time. Because number two fell in February (the week before Valentine's Day), and because one of our bullshit rah-rah IT Department mottos was *The Heart of IT*, we coupled bacon with chocolate (never a bad thing to do). So, there were plenty o' chocolate delights to complement Sir Bacon. And bonus, it was near my birthday, so Nellie Batt baked me an amazing Spicy Bacon cake. I might have had a few ~~giant~~ petite slices of that cake. It was my right.

BBBB2 brought a whole new spread of bacon-themed dishes, and, this round, people had ample time to think and prepare. We had new categories for voting and some new favorites included Smoked Salmon and Bacon Dip, Sweet and Spicy Bacon-Wrapped Pretzel Rods, and, my personal favorite, Chocolate Chip Cookie Brownie Bacon Bombs (thank you Obi Wan Fromobi, you know who you are). Honorable mention goes to Ben Honey for his Cheesy Bacon Potatoes presentation. Like Jane in BBBB1, he brought in a stuffed pig prop. If only we had kept her little pink piglet, there could have been porky love brewing.

But BBBB2 was not the end of it. Bacon lives on.

About a year after BBBB2, I started a private Facebook group *Where's My Bacon?* It is still active to this day.

Several years after the original Bring Back Bacon Buffet, my friend and coworker Mary Jo Darcy invited me to a Visualization Board workshop near Detroit. The workshop was led by a company employee named Gigi Tanner, one of the most positive and energetic women on this planet. I had never met Gigi in all my years with the company. I was not even technically a "company sister" any longer, having taken an opportunity as a consultant about six months before (though I will always consider myself a first cousin). Still, after 16 years at a job you do run into a lot of people, so when we arrived at the hotel conference room and began introductions, Gigi and I started trying to determine if we had crossed paths in the past. She did not seem to recognize my face, but, when Mary Jo introduced me as Beth Campbell, she cocked her head, thinking.

Gigi: "Your name sounds so familiar … how do I know you?"

Me: "Hmmm, did I meet you at the Women's Group kickoff last summer?"

Gigi: "No, I couldn't make that. Did you ever work at the North-west facility? I was there for a few years a while back."

Me: "Nope." I listed off a few more projects, all receiving a no from Gigi.

Gigi: "I know your name. This is going to drive me crazy!"

Me: [hesitantly] "Well, do you remember that bacon thing a few years ago … ?"

I didn't even finish the sentence. Her eyes got really big, and she exclaimed, "Oh my gosh, that was YOU? That was so great, I gotta give you a hug!"

And she did. Five years *AB* and she knew exactly what I was talking about. Even though she hadn't been commenting on the Yammer posts and her location didn't participate in the potluck, she still understood the power and expressed her acknowledgement with enthusiasm. I was beyond honored.

My niece Jane is a Goddess of Locks (a.k.a. cosmetologist) in the same city as the company headquarters. She told me she still occasionally gets clients from the company. Not unlike Gigi, they still very much remember the spirit of bacon and the events around the protest. Even for those who weren't actively involved in the social media or the buffet, it was powerful. In the grand scheme of things, it seems like such a small moment in company history, and yet it lives on.

When I left the company five years *AB*, I told *The Story of Bacon* to the new CIO Kevin at my going away party. Maya had "left" a couple of years prior, and Kevin had been hired to replace her. Kevin is very down to earth, tons of charisma, and connected with us in a way Maya never did. Look, I actually liked Maya in many ways. She's super smart, savvy, not unkind, and, anytime a woman is in a C-level position, I am applauding. But she was wrong for us—at least for the outsourcing effort. Her staff members were wrong for us. They didn't seem to be able to connect, they didn't try and earn our trust, and they didn't seem to trust us. I don't know if the outsourcing effort was her idea, something pitched after she got the job …

or if she was brought in specifically to make it happen. Either way, it just wasn't managed well. And I was not sad to see her go.

Kevin related much better to the masses, and I was beyond honored he showed up at my departure gathering. A few days earlier, he and I had been talking and somehow the Bacon Era came up. We didn't have time then, but I promised to tell the story at my party. There were a couple dozen people sitting around the big conference room table eating cake and ice cream while I told the tale. What really resonated was not that the CIO willingly showed up to say goodbye or that he was listening to our history and actually seemed engaged, but rather that so many of the other guests piped in with their memories of the time. This wasn't my story. It was their story. And it felt good to be able to talk about it years after the fact, openly … and still able to laugh at it all while at the same time not downplaying its significance. It felt like the passing of the baton. Bacon had been powerful, but now we passed on the legacy to the new leadership. And, in some small way, it felt like the message still resonated, a lesson learned that would prevent this from happening again.

Long live bacon.

Chapter 13

Recipes Inspired by the BBBB

During the Bring Back Bacon Buffet event, I asked participants to share their recipes so I could publish them to the rest of the company. It would be a crime to keep such treasures secret. The people who had tasted the bacon wonders might want to recreate the dishes on their own terms (i.e., add even more bacon and consume in private, when the kids are asleep and won't come whining for a bite). Also, the people who had not been able to participate in the potluck could have at least a small sampling of the magical bacon goodness that the rest of us enjoyed.

I received some great recipes from my Baconstituents. Unfortunately, many of them were less than precise and somewhat vague, so I have done my best to fill in the gaps and provide measurements when possible. A few of the good recipes were never shared, so I have had to "wing it" on those. My soulmate Sean and his hungry coworkers tested all of them, so, if they suck, it's his fault. Rest assured, even if they are not professional recipes, they are perfectly safe for human consumption.

For all of these recipes, I highly recommend using real bacon that you cook up yourself. In an extreme pinch—like if your spouse is in a panic because they forgot it was their turn to provide something on "Goody Day" at work and it's 9 p.m. the night before—you may use real bacon bits that come in a bag or jar precooked. Don't make it a habit.

If you use fake bacon bits, you are dead to me. Shut this book right now and give it to someone who respects the integrity of real fried pork. You might as well go vegan, and there isn't anything I can do to help you until you decide to give yourself over to Bacon completely. If you have already used Facon, then the only way to redeem yourself is by preparing each of the following recipes exactly as written (using only authentic pork) and then blogging about your crimes publicly. After you have completed them all and asked for forgiveness, you might be allowed to join the ranks of true Bacon lovers, but only as an intern. It will take a long time to get back in our good graces, so just use real bacon and avoid all of this madness.

Bacon Cheese Disco Ball

Ingredients

Two 8-oz. packages of cream cheese, room temperature (not the fat-free kind, I beg you. If you hate your guests this much, just put out a vegetable tray).

½ cup grated Parmesan Cheese

½ cup Mayonnaise

¼ cup green onions

1 lb. bacon, cooked, drained, and chopped finely

1 teaspoon salt

1/2 teaspoon pepper

Directions

Set half of the chopped bacon aside in a wide bowl or on a plate, preferably out of reach of hungry children and pets.

Mix the remaining ingredients together. Resist the urge to stick your finger into the mixture to sneak a bite prematurely. That is unacceptable (use a spoon, it's more sanitary). Shape this glob of goodness into something resembling a large ball. Roll the ball in the remaining bacon so it gets coated all over the outside like porky glitter.

Refrigerate for at least a couple hours prior to serving. Attempt to compose yourself while carrying it to the serving table and fight the temptation to put your face down in it and shamelessly take a large bite. Your guests will notice the cream cheese and bacon mustache.

Serve with a variety of quality crackers (or vegetables, I guess … but why?). Crank up some KC and the Sunshine Band as you take your first bite.

Mind-blowing Bacon Hash Brown Breakfast Bake

Leftovers for hours. Just sayin'.

1 bag hash browns—frozen (about 30 oz.)

2 lb. bacon, cooked, drained, and crumbled (minus a few strips because you know you will eat some while assembling this treasure).

1 lb. of your second favorite pork product, cooked, drained, and chopped (suggestions: ham, more bacon because why not, country sausage, pork belly).

24-30 eggs

1 cup milk or half-and-half (milk is fine, half-and-half makes it a bit richer).

2 green peppers, chopped (you can use yellow or red or orange if you prefer; we do not discriminate here).

1 large onion, chopped (skip these if you have weirdos in your family who do not like onions. Or put them in anyway and announce it to everyone. The weirdos won't eat the casserole, leaving more for you.)

4 cups extra-sharp cheddar cheese (a little extra if you have dogs and tend to "accidentally" drop some on the floor for them.)

1 tablespoon garlic powder

1 tablespoon onion powder

1 teaspoon salt

1 tablespoon pepper

Nonstick spray or butter or bacon grease to lube the pan

Preheat your oven to 350°F. Grease a 9 x 13-inch deep roasting pan with the leftover bacon grease or real butter (disposable aluminum roasters are perfect if you are worried about leaving your favorite dish at the neighbor's potluck where it conveniently never gets returned even though you wrote your name and phone number on the bottom with a Sharpie, thanks a lot, Linda). Yes, you can use nonstick spray. I get it. It's easy to use. But seriously … you just cooked up two pounds of bacon, why not take advantage of that leftover pork lard?

In a large bowl, whisk the eggs with the milk/half-and-half, garlic powder, onion powder, salt, and pepper. Use an electric mixer; it will be so much easier. There are a LOT of eggs. Set the bowl aside and give a moment of gratitude for that vat of breakfast gold.

Break up the frozen hash browns with a hammer or meat mallet if they are in a large frozen clump. Assemble your ingredients in a sacrificial circle around the greased roasting pan. Layer the ingredients in the pan in the following order (or just mix them all together in a giant bowl and pour into the pan):

1. Green peppers on the very bottom

2. Half of the frozen hash browns

3. Half the cheese (about 2 cups)

4. Half of the crumbled bacon and half of the other pork

5. Pause to wipe the drool from your chin

6. Onions

7. Remaining hash browns

8. Remaining cheese (2 cups)

9. Remaining bacon and other pork

Stop and admire this work of art.

Pour the egg mixture evenly over the top of the layers. Use a spoon or spatula or gravity to even out the liquid and make sure the dry ingredients get soaked. Smush everything down a bit if you have to.

Spray a piece of aluminum foil with non-stick spray (yes, I contradict myself) and place it loosely over the top of your creation. Bake for 45 minutes. Remove the foil and cook for an additional 30 minutes. Check the middle and see if it is done. If it's pretty runny, put it back in the oven for 10-minute increments until the center starts to set up. It will cook a bit upon removing from the oven so don't get into a panic. Cook it longer if you are paranoid; you really can't mess this one up. If it starts getting too brown on top for your liking, put the foil back on top. Or just stop being a baby and don't worry about it. Who's going to say anything? You just made a delicious bacon, sausage, egg, cheese, and hash brown masterpiece. If anyone complains that the top is too brown, pull their plate from under them and stab their overcooked hunk of breakfast bake with your fork to make your point. Break off a huge chunk and slowly put into your mouth as you stare at them like a maniac. Swallow and then drop your fork in a classic "Mic Drop" move. Good riddance to them, it just means there will be plenty for you to eat later when there's no one around and you want something comforting to nosh on while you watch your umpteenth season of Law and Order.

Let the casserole cool for 15 minutes or so before serving. You may want to just kick everyone (including yourself and the pets) out of the house and lock the doors, because this will be the longest 15 minutes of your life.

Tip from the husband's coworkers who taste-tested this recipe: even with all that amazing pork, hash browns can suck the life out of a dish. Feel free to apply Tabasco or Sriracha sauce liberally.

Bacon With Jalapeño Deviled Eggs

Ingredients

12 eggs
1 lb. or infinity slices of bacon
3-4 medium jalapeño peppers (NOT pronounced "juh-LAH-pin-ohs," someone please tell my husband this)
Mayonnaise (I can't measure this for you. Some people like their deviled egg mixture rough, some like it like soup. Start with 1/4–1/3 cup and add to your desired consistency.)
Mustard, 2 tablespoons or to taste (spicy brown or normal or whatever is your favorite)
Paprika
Salt & Pepper to taste

Directions

Boil or steam your eggs. I'm not going to tell you how to do it. Everyone has their "tried and true" method for perfect boiled eggs. I have tried them all, and they are all only *sometimes* true. None of them are 100 percent. So, cook your eggs in the shell however you normally prefer to do it. When done, run them under cold water or dunk them in a vat of ice water or whatever you need to do to get them cooled. Peel them, and pray to the egg gods you don't have one of those piece-of-shit eggs that doesn't want to peel and ends up being thrown across the room in anger. Allegedly.

Cook your bacon. Fry it in a skillet over medium-high heat or maybe in the oven. Get it fairly crispy but not burned. Or not. Make it how you love it. Drain the holy grail of foods on paper towels and put the leftover bacon grease in a jar and store in your fridge. The next time you make vegetables, sauté them in some hot bacon fat to make them edible. When the bacon is drained and cooled, coarsely chop or crumble it. Don't mince it. You want some good chunks in there.

Trim the stems off the ends of your jalapeños. Cut them in half and clean out the seeds. If you like a mild zip, leave a few seeds. If you are one of those daring folk who like to push the envelope of heat, leave a lot of seeds. If you remove them all, you'll have very little heat but you will get a nice smoky flavor. It's all good. Chop those suckers up pretty finely or, better yet, use a mini food processor if you are lazy like me. When you are done jalapeño chopping, wash your hands really well and avoid touching your eyes. Use disposable gloves if you think you might forget to be careful because that stuff will sting like a bitch.

Cut your eggs in half lengthwise and take out the yolk. Put those delicious centers into a bowl and mash them with a fork. Add the jalapeños, bacon, mustard, and mayonnaise, salt and pepper, and stir. Add mayonnaise and/or mustard as needed to your desired consistency. If you want, keep a couple tablespoons of the crumbled bacon aside to sprinkle on top of your masterpiece later on. I personally do not do this because, sometimes, it falls off, and then people at your party pick at the bacon pieces on the tray, leaving less for you to enjoy. I'm selfish that way, so I put all my bacon safely inside the yolk mixture.

If you like other crunchy shit in your deviled eggs, like onions, scallions, green peppers, or cheese, by all means add them. I am a purist, so I'll just stick with the peppers and God's gift of pork.

Tip: Do NOT attempt to substitute ranch dressing for the mayo. For the love of everything human, NO! Sean's grandma did that once, and it was not good.

Spoon the yolk-bacon-jalapeño mixture into the egg white halves. Dust with paprika. Sprinkle with your spare crumbled bacon if you are one of those people. Taste one, because you have to. It's your duty as a cook.

Tip: You should just double this recipe.

Now put 3–4 (or a half dozen) of those drool nuggets on a small plate, cover with your favorite wrap, and hide those suckers in the back of the fridge where no one can find them. You will thank me later. Plate up the rest and head to the party. Start your timer and watch how fast they disappear.

Bacon Crack Cornflake Cookies

Ingredients

1 cup butter—softened (two sticks, and none of that margarine crap)
¾ cup sugar
½ cup brown sugar
2 large eggs
1 ¾ cups all-purpose flour
1 teaspoon baking soda
1 teaspoon REAL vanilla extract
1 lb. bacon, cooked, drained, and crumbled (feel free to double this, don't mind if I do).
4 cups of your favorite cornflake cereal, crushed
1 12-oz. bag of milk chocolate chips
1 cup dried cherries

OK, if you are not a cornflake fan, then A) who are you, and B) you could substitute some other awesome cereal like Rice Chex or Cinnamon Toast Crunch. All good. Also, if you are one of those weirdos who prefers dark or semi-sweet chocolate, it's your call. Not my preference—in fact, I'd suggest half milk chocolate, half white chocolate chips if you are really daring—but I'll forgive you in this case, because you incorporated bacon into a cookie without fear, and, for that, I salute you.

Directions

Preheat your oven to 375°F. Mix the flour and baking soda in a bowl. In a separate bowl, beat the butter, sugar, brown sugar, and vanilla extract until it's nice and creamy. Make sure the second bowl is big enough for all of the goodness, because you're going to need the room. Add eggs, one at a time, beat well after each one. Add in the flour mixture a little at a time and, good grief, turn your mixer speed down first otherwise you're going to be cleaning flour off your cupboards for days. Mix until blended.

Stir in the cornflakes, bacon, chocolate chips, and dried cherries. You can do this by hand if you're a classic baker or by machine/hand mixer if you are smart and lazy like me. Warning: you're going to need to jack up the power level here.

Option: you could use raisins instead of dried cherries. Raisins are cool. I don't hate them. I just prefer the sweet/tart of dried cherries, and I've gotten accustomed to using them instead of raisins because my husband thinks raisins are gross, so we don't go there.

Drop the mixed dough in rounded tablespoons onto ungreased baking sheets. If they aren't perfectly rounded, don't panic. You don't have to roll these. If your "rounded tablespoons" look more like a piece of cement that fell off a building, never fear, they will turn out just fine.

Bake for 9 to 11 minutes. I know at this point most cookie recipes say something like "bake until golden brown." If you like a firmer cookie, by all means, follow the standard. If you like a more soft and chewy disk, bake them just until they start getting a teeeensy bit golden on top. Take them out and let them sit on the pan for a few minutes to finish cooking. When they are just firm enough to not collapse into a singularity when you put a spatula underneath them, transfer to a cooling rack or some wax paper on the counter (or just the counter—I've done it for years, and no one has died). When the cookies have cooled a bit more and are starting to get rigid, throw some of them onto a plate or platter in a single layer and put them in the freezer. Every five minutes or so, you can pile on another layer of cookies without fear of them sticking because they will be frozen on the outside. This will help keep them nice and soft.

Store your cookies in the fridge if you are using them soon or in the freezer if you are saving them for another occasion—and, if you are one of those people who actually *can* save cookies in your freezer for an extended period, I bow to your will power; you can probably also put out a bowl of candy on your desk for your coworkers and not eat 90 percent of it yourself before the end of the day … good for you, my unicorn. Storing cookies in the cold helps keep them nice and soft and chewy. It only takes a short time to thaw out a frozen cookie (so I am told by people who actually have that kind of mental strength) and it's worth it.

As we have mentioned before, I am quite lazy, so I often do a "brownie" version of cookie recipes instead of undertaking the painstaking ordeal of scooping multiple batches of individual discs. Plus, I generally consume less raw dough with the pan-cookie model, which means less intestinal gas and more cooked product to consume later. If you, like me, have a verbal gut reaction to too much raw cookie dough, you may want to use this alternative.

Preheat oven to 350°F. Liberally butter a 9 x 13-inch cake pan. Mix up the cookie dough as above. Spread into the buttered pan like you are making love to it. It is perfectly OK if you accidentally end up with a thick coating of cookie dough on the back of the spoon. That stuff is bad for your sink, so you'll have to lick it off before you do the dishes. Bake for 20 to 25 minutes until it just starts to get golden brown on top. Let cool completely, then cut. Store in the fridge or freezer (see above). Makes about two brownies or two dozen, depending on what you consider a respectable serving.

Consume with real cow's milk. Seriously, you used real butter for this; don't wimp out now.

Chocolate-covered Bacon Bliss

Ingredients

Two (2) 1-lb. packages of thick-cut bacon, cooked crisp and cooled, cut in half

16 oz. semisweet or milk chocolate chips (you can use the bar chocolate, too, chopped).

8 oz. white chocolate (same as above).

Directions

Melt both the semisweet (or milk) chocolate and white chocolate in separate double boilers. No one owns a double boiler anymore except your grandma, so just place a heat-proof bowl on top of a pan of simmering water. Two bowls, two pans. Stir with a whisk or spatula until well-melted and smooth. Remove from the heat.

You may be asking yourself if using a microwave is an acceptable alternative. If you live in a studio apartment with a broken stove or one that looks like the last four tenants grilled directly onto the burner and never cleaned it off, then by all means you can use the microwave to melt your chocolate. You'll have to be careful lest you risk your chocolate being overcooked and mushy rather than smoothly melted. But, really, how bad would it be if you had to spread the chocolate onto your bacon halves rather than dip the bacon into the chocolate? Not bad, really. In fact, if you are super lazy, just skip this recipe altogether. Pop a few chocolate chips into your mouth, bite into a slice of bacon, and it's basically the same thing.

But, if presentation is a concern, then use a double boiler. You just have more control that way.

Line a cookie sheet or other flat, tray-like dish with wax paper. Dip your thick bacon half-strips into the melted semisweet chocolate. Really, drown is a better word. Drown your bacon in the chocolate, then put it on the wax paper to cool. Repeat with all the bacon slices. Drizzle the melted white chocolate over the strips (or, as an alternative, cool them first and double-dip the ends into the white chocolate). Put the strips in the refrigerator to cool for about a half hour.

If there are any left by the time your guests arrive, put them on a pretty plate and serve.

Bacon Tater Casserole #Cheesy

Ingredients

2 cans condensed cream of potato soup (I do recommend Campbell's, but, then again … I am biased).

2 cups sour cream (Daisy brand is my favorite).

2 bags of shredded cheese (Four cups total, use whatever kind you like; sharp cheddar works well, or the Mexican blend).

1 bag (about 30 oz.) frozen cubed or shredded hash browns, (another award-winning appearance by hash browns! Who knew?)

1 tablespoon garlic powder

1 tablespoon onion powder

2 cups bacon, cooked, drained, and crumbled (or chopped).

1 cup grated parmesan or asiago cheese (to sprinkle on top).

Nonstick spray, butter, or bacon grease to lube the pan

Directions

Pre-heat oven to 350°F. Grease or spray a 9 x 13-inch baking dish.

Set aside one cup of the shredded cheese, all the grated parmesan (or asiago), and about one-third cup of the bacon; we will use those later. I like asiago better than parmesan, although, until about six months ago, I pronounced it "uh-SAH-jee-oh." Then, one day at Panera, I ordered an *uh-SAH-jee-oh* bagel and the grandmotherly cashier corrected me … IN AN ITALIAN ACCENT. "Ah-see-AH-go," she said, and she actually put up her finger like she was scolding me. So, pronounce it right or risk public humiliation by Nonna at your local Panera.

Mix the remaining ingredients together in a large bowl. Add the mixture to the greased baking dish and even out with a spoon or spatula. Resist the urge to lick the spatula, or at least make sure no one is watching when you do. Wait until the very end so you don't get your saliva in the paragon of pork; that's gross. Top this amazing creation with the remaining cheeses and sprinkle with the reserved bacon.

Bake for 45 minutes or until the top is the color of a quality spray tan and the taters are fork tender. If needed, bake for another 10-15 minutes. You could also do this in a slow cooker on low for six to eight hours.

For that matter, the possibilities are endless. Use a different condensed soup (cream of mushroom, cream of chicken); add real onions, green peppers, hot peppers, whatever crunchy shit you like in your taters, different spices, maybe a dash of cayenne pepper or some dill. Collapse in ecstasy and take a long nap.

Incredible Tuna (or Chicken) Salad With Bacon

This is a recipe for people who do not like to measure. I am not one of those people. Last Christmas, I couldn't find the family meatball recipe, so I emailed my sister Allison to get it from her. She responded with the ingredients for both the meatballs and the delightful brown-sugar sauce ... *sans quantities*. I responded, "WTF DO YOU EXPECT ME TO DO WITH THIS, DO YOU KNOW WHO YOU ARE TALKING TO, BITCH?" OK, what I really said was, "Um, do you have the actual recipe, with the amounts?" to which she replied, "Oh, right, I forgot. It might kill you to wing something. Silly me; what was I thinking?" Bless her heart; she found the actual recipe for me. That's what sisters do for each other. They look past anal-retentive personality traits.

If you are the type of person who puts a spreadsheet together to research dog food or manage your gardening, then I feel for you. Like me, you will have to overcome this challenge and "wing it." Never fear; it's all good. Like some of the other recipes, it's hard to mess this one up.

Three 5-oz. cans of tuna packed in water (you could use chicken as well—about 16 oz. canned, roasted, poached, or whatever. I get it ... some people hate tuna. No shame).

1 lb. Bacon, cooked, drained, and chopped

3 large "dollops" of mayo or Miracle Whip (I can't tell you which is better. I like both mayo and MW, so pull up your adult pants and just choose one or use both. This is probably about a cup, but hell if I know. It's all about preference).

Roughly 2 cups shredded cheese, whatever flavor you like

A good-sized handful of chopped celery (feel free to skip this if you, like me, hate celery in your salads. It makes no sense. I cannot explain it. I am OK with onions or peppers, so it's not a texture thing. And celery doesn't gross me out or anything. It's just not my thing).

A good-sized handful of chopped onion (I prefer green onions, but I have never made this with green onions, so let me know how it turns out).

Some cherry or grape tomatoes

½–¾ lb. shell pasta, cooked per package instructions (you can use small or medium shells or any pasta shape you like. Shells are good, because they act like little fairy cups to hold the creamy tuna-bacon deliciousness. But I also like bowtie pasta, regular macaroni, and those little curly ones).
Fresh or dried dill
Salt and pepper to taste

Mix it all together in a big bowl. Serve. God, I love easy recipes. This bacon tuna pasta salad extraordinaire makes a great breakfast, lunch, dinner, or snack.

This was one of the few recipes I did not send to work with Sean for his coworkers to test. It was too damn good. He and I ate the whole thing. It just got better and better every day.

Sensational Sesame Noodles With Bacon Chaser

This recipe will make enough to throw in a standard slow cooker to keep warm for an intimate family gathering (or about four servings in the Campbell household; we do like our American-sized portions). Double this recipe for an extra-large slow cooker, or if you have a big brother like I did (RIP Big Joe) who might go through half a pound of this as a side dish.

The Sensational Sesame/Peanut Butter Sauce—Ingredients

½ cup smooth peanut butter (I have used both name-brand PB and the natural kind that you have to stir, both work fine).
¼ cup soy sauce
⅓ cup warm water
3-4 medium garlic cloves, minced or pressed (use more if you like to burp into your spouse's face after dinner while sitting on the couch, and they will have no idea what is about to hit them).
2 tablespoons red-wine vinegar
2-3 tablespoons sesame oil (I go a little generous on this as I like the flavor).
2 teaspoons honey
1 teaspoon dried hot red pepper flakes

The Noodles—Ingredients

1 box of your favorite long, skinny pasta (spaghetti, thin spaghetti, angel hair, linguini, whatever you like).
2 bunches of green onions sliced thin (about ½ cup).
1 cup of chopped peppers (about two peppers, any color).
3 tablespoons toasted sesame seeds (you can buy them already toasted but they are very easy to toast by hand, instructions below).

The Chaser

2 lbs. bacon, cooked and chopped coarsely

Sauce—Directions

Have a large bowl or slow cooker handy (slow cooker on warm).

Put all dressing ingredients in a blender and blend until smooth, usually takes a minute or two. Make sure it's really blended, or you might accidentally bite into a red pepper flake or get one caught in the back of your throat. Pour your blended sauce into a large bowl or straight into the slow cooker.

Noodles—Directions

Toast the sesame seeds in a dry pan over medium heat until they just start to get brown. Shake the pan while cooking. Do that tossing thing the professional chefs do. If you can do that, you are the Supreme Deity of sesame seed toasting. If not, just shake the pan back and forth and/or stir its contents for a minute or so; they will toast very quickly. Swipe the seeds into a cool bowl, plate, or paper towel so they don't continue to cook.

Cook pasta according to directions. Drain. Add the pasta, green onions, peppers, and toasted sesame seeds to the bowl or slow cooker with the sauce. Mix well. A pasta fork (or two) really comes in handy here. Sprinkle in salt and pepper to taste.

Serve in a mountain-sized mound on a plate, sprinkle or toss with bacon, then inhale that most supreme offering to the Flying Spaghetti Monster and prepare to undo your pants in about 20 minutes.

Tip: Add some chicken breast or shrimp with the bacon.

Another tip: The sauce can be used solo with chicken or shrimp or for dipping your egg rolls. *Mmmm.*

Maple Bacon Cupcakes with Maple Bacon Frosting

Makes about 18 normal-people cupcakes (or six servings in my family).

The Cupcakes - Ingredients

2 ½ cups all-purpose flour
1 teaspoon baking soda
2 teaspoons baking powder
½ teaspoon salt
½ cup (1 stick) actual butter, softened
¾ cup brown sugar (dark or light? Does it really matter? No, it
  does not).
2 large eggs
1 cup pure maple syrup (do not for one millisecond think you can cheap
  out on this and use commercial pancake syrup. Is that how you treat
  bacon? Are you really a patriot? Use REAL maple syrup. If you can't
  swing that, then step away from the kitchen and let your grandmother
  figure this out.)
2 teaspoons REAL vanilla extract (you know how I feel about this).
½ cup half-and-half or milk
1 lb. bacon, cooked and chopped finely
1 teaspoon cinnamon

Directions

Preheat oven to 350°F. Place liners in your muffin tin if you're going all ho-
ity-toity with your cupcakes, otherwise spray the tin with non-stick spray
or butter liberally.

Sift together the flour, baking powder, baking soda, salt. If you don't have
a sifter, use a fine sieve, or just mix together with a spoon or spatula and
don't worry too much about it. Put the mixture aside.

In a large bowl, beat the butter, vanilla, and brown sugar together on medium speed until the mixture is fluffy enough that you cannot avoid stick-

ing your finger in there and tasting it. Add the eggs, half-and-half, and REAL maple syrup. Beat well. Get out your aggression Julia Child style.

Gradually add the flour mixture to the butter mixture, but turn down the speed lest you look like an extra from *Scarface*. Fill the muffin cups/liners about two-thirds full, then sprinkle a little of the chopped bacon on top of each. Bake until a toothpick comes out clean, about 20 minutes for normal-sized cupcakes (11–13 minutes for the minis). Let those little wonders cool completely, and don't allow yourself to consume any of them unfrosted. These are cupcakes, not muffins.

The Frosting - Ingredients

1 cup (2 sticks) unsalted butter
4 oz. cream cheese, softened (half a brick, use the rest on a bagel or mix it with sugar and pretend it's cheesecake).
¾ cup brown sugar
1/4 tsp. salt
1/3 cups REAL maple syrup (emphasis in case you didn't get this the first time).
1 tsp. REAL vanilla extract
1 ½ teaspoons maple extract (even though this is imitation and goes against my core values in baking, you really need this to get that good maple flavor).
3–4 cups confectioners' sugar
1 lb. bacon, cooked and crumbled
Course sugar crystals for decorating (optional, but they really do make the cupcakes look like a professional did them).

Directions

In a large bowl, beat the butter, cream cheese, brown sugar, vanilla, maple extract, and salt, on medium speed for two to three minutes until well thrashed. While continuing to beat, add the REAL maple syrup. Turn the mixer down a tad and start adding the confectioners' sugar a little at a time. Once everything is fully incorporated and the risk of a four-foot sugar spread is mitigated, crank that sucker up too high, and beat until light and fluffy for a minute or so.

If your frosting is still a little on the soft side, pop it in the fridge for 30 minutes or so.

If you are serving these to others, use a piping bag with a cool swirly tip to apply the frosting to the cooled cupcakes. Apply a sprinkle of crumbled bacon to the top, and then add a dusting of coarse sugar crystals so it looks like your bacon is swimming in a sea of diamonds.

If you are not serving these to outsiders, blob a big spoonful of frosting on top of the cupcake, smush some crumbled bacon into it, and add a tea-spoon of coarse sugar crystals because it looks pretty and there is no such thing as "too sweet." Put it in a bowl (without the liner) and fill the bowl halfway up with milk. Eat this mound of rapture with a fork, like a slice of cake. Yes, in the milk, like it's a cereal cupcake. That's how we roll in my family.

Bitchin' Bacon Buckeyes

Ingredients

1 cup (2 sticks) butter, softened

1 ½ cups peanut butter (DO NOT use the natural stuff here; a good buckeye requires peanut butter with the consistency of Play-Doh, so don't go all raw beets and granola on this one).

1 teaspoon REAL vanilla extract

6 cups confectioner's sugar

4 cups (2 bags) chocolate chips (traditionally, semi-sweet but feel free to go milk chocolate. Or super dark chocolate if you are one of those freaks).

2 lbs bacon, cooked, drained, and chopped well

Directions

In a large bowl, mix together the peanut butter, actual butter, REAL vanilla extract, and confectioner's sugar. It will look pretty dry; this is normal. Roll into balls about one-inch in diameter. A melon ball scoop helps here, to get a consistent size. But don't fret it if you have to use a normal spoon; they will taste just as magnificent, even if they are shaped like a trapezoid. Put your Buckeye Balls on cookie sheets lined with wax paper. Insert a tooth-pick into each ball (that's what she said) and then put them into the freezer for a half hour or so. Go watch an episode of *The Office*. Any episode, doesn't matter. US or UK, both fabulous.

Melt the chocolate chips in a double boiler (a.k.a., a bowl suspended over a pan of simmering water). Stir often until all the chips are melted.

Pull the peanut butter balls out of the freezer. Put the chopped bacon in a bowl. Using the toothpicks as a handle, dip the balls into the melted chocolate until almost covered, but leave a little at the top showing so they look like real buckeyes (not the Ohio State people, as I have explained earlier). Immediately dip the bottom into the chopped bacon. Put the dipped balls back on the wax-covered cookie sheet. When the pan is full, put in the fridge.

Once they are cooled completely and hardened, you can pack them away in a container and store in the fridge or freezer. So what if a few of them stick together? Would it really be a crime if you pulled out one and two more came along with it? You WANT that to happen.

Hamburger & Beans with Bacon

Don't get all freaked out. I'm not going to make you cook beans from scratch. I would never in a million bazillion years do that to you. There are so many wonderful bean companies that have done all the hard work for us already.

This recipe is actually a family heirloom, having been a staple in our Midwestern home starting in the late '70s. A couple of the bacon buffet recipes were similar to this, without the beans. You might be thinking, well, I could omit the beans, too. You could, if you are a total loser, because then it wouldn't be Hamburger & Beans, would it? If you want to make a recipe called Hamburger & Something-Other-Than-Beans With Bacon, then go for it. But you can't use this recipe unless you give your word you will use beans.

That being said, you can ADD whatever you want. This dish lends itself to infinite varieties. My sister Susan makes the classic version, the one I remember so much from my childhood. It has no potatoes and (HORROR!) no bacon. But, if you want something quick, simple is the way to go. My sister Allison goes all out with potatoes and brown sugar. She has to bulk it up with spuds, because she has a lot of kids to feed.

This version is destined to be the new favorite. The addition of fried pork bits takes it over the edge into the realm of mythology.

Ingredients

1 lb. bacon
1 lb. ground beef (80 percent fat content or higher, come on! Fat makes things taste GOOD).
1–2 16-oz. cans baked beans (almost any variety works here; Susie says she uses Bush's maple cured bacon beans … and why NOT? The more bacon, the better).

2 cups potatoes, cooked and cut into chunks (this recipe is great for leftover spuds, you can use almost anything here—baked, boiled, steamed, roasted, hash browns, etc).

1 medium onion, chopped

1 tablespoon crushed or minced garlic

¼ cup brown sugar (use less if you hate sweet, more if you love it).

1 tablespoon garlic powder

Salt and pepper, to taste

Directions

Over medium heat, in a large frying pan, cook the bacon in batches. Drain on paper towels and try not to sneak TOO many slices for yourself (optional: fry up 2 lbs. of bacon and eat 1 lb. yourself while putting this award-winner together).

Leave the burner on while you pour the excess bacon grease into your bacon grease jar. I assume you have one sitting in your fridge and have nicknamed it "My PRECIOUS!" Leave a bit of a bacon glaze at the bottom of the pan; it will contribute to the flavor. Add the ground beef, onions, and garlic. Stir and fry until the meat is fully cooked. Drain the fat as needed (but NOT into the bacon grease jar).

Add the bacon, potatoes, beans, brown sugar, garlic powder, and salt/pepper to taste. Stir well. When everything is heated thoroughly, it's ready to eat. Warning: you may need a spoon AND a fork to consume this beast.

Ooh La La L'bacon French Toast Casserole

You can double the recipe and use a deep roasting pan if feeding more than two people.

The Casserole—Ingredients

1 large loaf French bread (enough to fill a 9 x 13-inch pan; almost any robust bread will do here).
8 large eggs
2 cups half-and-half (or heavy cream if you like it rich).
1 cup milk
¼ cup granulated sugar
1–2 lbs. bacon, cooked, drained, and chopped
1 teaspoon vanilla extract
1 teaspoon ground cinnamon
Dash of salt
Butter (for greasing the pan).
Streusel Topping, recipe follows

Directions

Generously … and I mean GENEROUSLY … butter a 13 x 9-inch baking dish (glass or metal). You will thank yourself not only when consuming this amazing dish but afterward, when it isn't all crusted to the sides.

Cut or tear bread into cubes, about one-inch wide. Arrange evenly in the baking dish.

In a large bowl, combine the eggs, half-and-half or cream, milk, sugar, vanilla, cinnamon, and salt. Beat with a mixer until blended but not super frothy (you can use a whisk if you're really trying to get the biceps tightened up, Powerhouse). Pour the egg mixture over the bread chunks, making sure they are all covered evenly. I like to toss a bit and then press lightly to get all the bread saturated. Cover with foil and refrigerate overnight. Put the chopped bacon in a re-sealable bag and store in the refrigerator overnight.

Hide the bag in an opaque container labeled "Chicken Liver & Beets" so no one will go near it.

Now, make the streusel topping so you are all prepped in the morning.

Streusel Topping—Ingredients

1 cup (2 sticks) cold butter
1 cup packed light brown sugar
1/2 teaspoon ground cinnamon
½ cup flour

Directions

Cut the butter into small pieces and place in a large bowl. Add flour, brown sugar, and cinnamon. Cut with pastry cutter or just smush it up with your hands. Add more flour if the mixture is too pasty; you want it to be crumbly and the butter mostly mixed in. Put in a re-sealable bag or storage container and refrigerate.

The next day, preheat oven to 350°F.

Toss the bread/egg mixture once more to evenly coat. Most of the liquid will be soaked into the bread at this point. Sprinkle the bacon evenly over the top (or concentrate a bunch in one corner and make sure to remember which corner it is so you can make that your portion). Spread the Streusel Topping evenly over the top and bake for 40 minutes until puffed and lightly golden. For a double-sized recipe, bake for a full hour. If edges get too brown too quickly, cut out the middle of a rectangle piece of foil and lay on top to let the middle continue to brown. Let it sit for 10 minutes or so, then consume like it's your last meal.

Tip: Sprinkle even more crushed bacon bits on top before serving, mmmmm. Or serve with a little maple syrup drizzled on top. Or both!

Tip: make this the night before your breakfast or brunch; store in the fridge and pop into the oven in the a.m.

Bacon Smothered in Jalapeño Cornbread

This is a sweet cornbread with some salt & spice, but, if you are one of those oddballs who doesn't like sweet cornbread, then you can cut down on the sugar.

NOTE: several of Sean's coworkers voted this the "Best of the Bacon" recipes. I don't like to play favorites, but it was amazing.

Ingredients

1 ½ sticks real butter, softened

2/3 cup brown sugar (use one-third cup if you like less sweet, one cup if you want your teeth to rot—no shame, brothers and sisters).

2 cups cornmeal

1 1/2 cups AP flour

4 teaspoons baking powder

1 teaspoon salt

3 large eggs

1 cup sour cream

1 ½ cups half-and-half

1 cup Jalapeño peppers, chopped (remove seeds if you want smoky but not hot; leave in seeds for more FIRE, BABY!)

1 lb. bacon, cooked, drained, chopped

Another ½ stick real butter for the dish

Directions

Preheat oven to 400°F. GENEROUSLY (are you getting my meaning here?) grease a 9x13-inch glass or metal baking dish. Really slather it on.

Beat butter and brown sugar together in a large bowl until smooth. In a separate bowl mix the cornmeal, AP flour, baking powder, and salt. Set aside. Crack the eggs into a medium bowl. Add the half-and-half and sour cream, whisk until well-combined and just a little bubbly. This next part do with a very slow mixer or by hand: pour a little of the flour mixture and a little of the egg/half-and-half/sour cream mixture into the butter-brown sugar bowl, mixing just until incorporated. Repeat several times until all of the egg and flour mixtures are incorporated. Fold in the Jalapeño peppers and bacon by hand. Spread this golden lava into the buttered 9 x 13-inch dish.

Bake your masterpiece until a toothpick or knife inserted into the center comes out clean, 24 minutes give or take. Let cool for 10 minutes before devouring with even more butter.

Bacon Cornbread For Lazy People

If you are lucky enough to live in a part of the world where you can buy the amazing Jiffy cornbread mix, this will save you some time from above. If you like your cornbread on the dry, crumbly side (many do), just follow the recipe on the box exactly and add the bacon. It will be quite delightful.

I prefer my cornbread moist, almost like cake. One of my favorite BBQ restaurants serves Jiffy cornbread on the side and it's wonderfully soft, just how I like it. I asked our server one day how they made it so delightful. She told me they added butter and sour cream. So, this is basically the recipe on the back of the box but with butter and sour cream. And bacon, because HELL to the YES.

Ingredients

2 boxes Jiffy Corn Muffin Mix
2 large eggs
2/3 cups half-and-half (you can use milk, but I like it richer).
1 cup sour cream
1 stick butter, melted
1 jar REAL bacon bits (if you use the imitation kind, I will call the cops. Of COURSE you can use bacon you cook up yourself. The inclusion of real bacon bits from a jar or bag is just to help out the sluggish of the world, that's why it's called "Bacon Cornbread for Lazy People.")
More butter for the pan

Directions

Preheat the oven to 400°F. Generously butter a 9 x 13-inch baking dish (metal or glass).

Mix all ingredients except bacon in a large bowl by hand with a wooden spoon, spatula, or large whisk. The batter will be lumpy; don't freak out. Fold in the chopped bacon. Let the batter sit for a few minutes while you clean up your filthy mess, you slob. Or eat some of the extra bacon you cooked, because you knew you would tap into that sizzling embodiment of awesome.

Pour batter into the buttered pan. Bake for 30 minutes, give or take, until golden brown. Pay respect to the Jiffy gods and all pigs by closing your eyes and licking your lips before you take your first bite.

Just Bacon

1 lb. hickory-smoked (or applewood-smoked or whatever-smoked) bacon
1 plate
Paper towels

<u>Directions</u>

Close your curtains and lock your doors.

Fry bacon in a pan over a hot burner or in the oven or over some glowing coals. Drain on paper towels. Eat. You're welcome.

Chapter 14

Ode To Bacon

Bacon, how do I love thee? Let me count the ways:
I love thee in BLT's on warm summer days;
I love thee in omelets and eggs scrambled hot;
I love thee in chili I cook in a pot;
I love thee on burgers and salads so green;
On top or on bottom, or somewhere between;
I love thee on pancakes with syrup on top;
I melt at your sizzle, your sweet fatty "pop!"
I love thee at breakfast or supper or lunch;
Or covered with chocolate for a sugary punch;
I love thee in muffins or big cheesy balls;
I love thee when pan-fried, grease spattered on walls;
I love thee on pizza that's piled up with cheese;
I love thee on 'taters, with sour cream, please;
In quiches with spinach I love thee as such;
And wrapped 'round a shrimp, oh I love thee so much!
In infinite ways is your flavor a treat;
Oh bacon, I love thee, and can't wait to eat!

Acknowledgements

First and foremost, I want to thank my awesome husband Sean for bearing with my constant bacon references while I was writing this book. He also gets a boatload of gratitude for being my guinea pig, testing out the recipes I had to piece together from vague BBBB contributions. He was a trooper, hauling my creations to his workplace so I could get some feedback. I just wanted to make sure the recipes didn't suck or kill people, but he was able to get some solid pointers that helped me refine a few of them. Thank you, dear heart … doing anything with you always feels like home.

Thank you to my family for your undying support, especially my siblings Abdul "Big Joe" (RIP, you inspire me even from beyond the grave), Steve, Keith, Susan, Allison, and Chris. You are always on my mind when I am thinking about or writing about food of any kind. Thank you, Allison, for your ambiguous recipes; thank you Sue for following up those ambiguous recipes with the actual ingredient quantities. You all are my living bacons and I love you.

Thank you to my friend and inspiration Kori Jo Bennett, for coaching me through some tough times at my day job while I was trying to put this together, and for always being a positive voice of encouragement in my pursuit of dreams. Change the channel. Be the magnet. I fucking love you, girl.

This story wouldn't be possible without so many people from my former job, the hundreds of people who weighed in on the bacon trauma in one way or the other. Special love going out to Chris D., Brad S., Amy N., Craig H., Mitch R., Nora B., and Saudia S. for your particularly inspiring input into the event. Thank you and the rest of the Baconeers for being so passionate about fried pork.

And finally, thank you to the person behind it all, "Darrin Potter." If it were not for your post, none of this would have happened. Thank you for posting (and then reposting) your bacon lament. It was a sad day for bacon, but we managed to bring a little happy into the workplace if but for a fleeting moment.

About the Author

Beth Anne Campbell is an IT consultant and manager who has worked in the corporate world for two decades. Born and raised in the state of Michigan, she is currently living in Virginia with her husband, Sean. She describes herself as "slightly rebellious, harmlessly sarcastic, and passionate about good leadership." In her spare time, she can be found working on her next blog or book, hiking the beautiful Blue Ridge Mountains' trails, or spending time with her extended family of five siblings and 13 nieces and nephews.

As a writer, Beth has learned to recognize events that are worth putting down on paper. She realized the "bacon story" was important while it was happening and captured the events in her personal journal at the end of each day. She knew, someday, she would share the tale of how bacon became the voice of the people and a beacon of change.